The Widow's Comfort

The Widow's Comfort

Navigating the Loss of Life's Most Treasured Relationship

By
Frank R. Shivers

Copyright 2022 by
Frank Shivers Evangelistic Association
All rights reserved
Printed in the United States of America

Unless otherwise noted, Scripture quotations are from
The Holy Bible *King James Version*

Library of Congress Cataloging-in-Publication Data

Shivers, Frank R., 1949-
The Widow's Comfort / Frank Shivers
ISBN 978-1-878127-48-8

Library of Congress Control Number:
2022904936

Cover design by
Tim King

For Information:
Frank Shivers Evangelistic Association
P. O. Box 9991
Columbia, South Carolina 29290
www.frankshivers.com

Dear refuge of my weary soul,
    On Thee, when sorrows rise,
On Thee, when waves of trouble roll,
    My fainting hope relies.

To Thee I tell each rising grief,
    For Thou alone canst heal.
Thy Word can bring a sweet relief
    For every pain I feel.

But, oh! when gloomy doubts prevail,
    I fear to call Thee mine.
The springs of comfort seem to fail,
    And all my hopes decline.

Yet, gracious God, where shall I flee?
    Thou art my only trust,
And still my soul would cleave to Thee,
    Though prostrate in the dust.—Anne Steele (1760)

Scriptures taken from the Holy Bible, New International Version®, NIV®, copyright © 1973, 1978, 1984, 2011 by Biblica, Inc.™ used by permission of Zondervan. All rights reserved worldwide. www.zondervan.com. The "NIV" and "New International Version" are trademarks registered in the United States Patent and Trademark Office by Biblica, Inc.™

Scripture quotations marked (NLT) are taken from the Holy Bible, New Living Translation, copyright ©1996, 2004, 2015 by Tyndale House Foundation, used by permission of Tyndale House Publishers, Carol Stream, Illinois 60188. All rights reserved.

Scripture quotations marked (TLB) are taken from The Living Bible, copyright © 1971, used by permission of Tyndale House Publishers, Carol Stream, Illinois 60188. All rights reserved.

Scripture quotations marked (NCV) are taken from the New Century Version®, copyright © 2005 by Thomas Nelson, used by permission. All rights reserved.

Scripture quotations marked (AMPC) are taken from the Amplified® Bible, copyright © 1954, 1958, 1962, 1964, 1965, 1987 by The Lockman Foundation, used by permission. www.lockman.org.

Scripture quotations marked (AMP) are taken from the Amplified® Bible, copyright © 2015 by The Lockman Foundation, used by permission. www.lockman.org.

Quotations marked (ESV) are taken from the Holy Bible, English Standard Version, copyright 2001 by Crossway, a publishing ministry of Good News Publishers, used by permission.

Publications by Frank R. Shivers

"We are not writing upon water but carving upon imperishable material."[1] ~ C. H. Spurgeon

The Treasure of Grace

Persecuted for Christ's Sake

When Things Just Don't Make Sense

When the Rain Comes

Christian Basics 101

Grief Beyond Measure, but Not Beyond Grace

Grief Beyond Measure, but Not Beyond Grace (Funeral Home Version)

Growing Old, Honorably and Happily

The Wounded Spirit

The Wounded Spirit: Companion Workbook

Growing in Knowledge, Living by Faith

Marriage and Parenting Boosters

Caught Up to Heaven

Expositions of the Psalms (Three Volumes)

Life Principles from Proverbs

The Evangelism Apologetic Study Bible

Hot Buttons on Apologetics

Hot Buttons on Morality

Hot Buttons on Discipleship

The Pornography Trap

The Poison of Porn

Heavy Stuff

Heavy Stuff (Student Workbook)

Clear Talk to Students

Nuggets of Truth (Three Volumes)

Soulwinning 101

Spurs to Soulwinning

Evangelistic Preaching 101

Evangelistic Praying

The Evangelistic Invitation 101

The Minister and the Funeral

Revivals 101

Children Sermons That Connect

Be Careful Little Eyes

How to Preach Without Evangelistic Results (Pamphlet)

False Hopes of Heaven (Tract)

First Steps for New Believers (Tract)

The Goal Line Stand (Tract)

The Death Clock (Tract)

The Widow's Comfort

To

the anguished,
devastated, lonely, afraid,
mourning and grieving widow:

May God
Wipe the tears away,
Mend the brokenness,
Fill the emptiness,
Calm the anxiousness,
Relieve the fearfulness,
Instill bright hopefulness,
Grant renewed meaningfulness,
And give you

"Beauty for ashes,
the oil of joy for mourning,
the garment of praise
for the spirit of heaviness."
—Isaiah 61:3

"When the husband of earth is removed, the godly widow casts herself upon the care of her Maker."[2]—C. H. Spurgeon

Contents

Preface

Introduction

  1 A Widow's Grief

  2 The Widow's Care

  3 Death, the Threshold to Something Better

  4 Grieving Isn't Craziness

  5 Coping with Your Feelings

  6 Basic Essentials for Healing

  7 Moving On Is Not Forgetting or Betraying Him

  8 Dark Yesterdays and Todays Become Bright Tomorrows

  9 Alligators and Grief

10 Not a Tear Goes Unnoticed

11 Healing through Memories

12 Bethany Is No Longer Bethany

13 Consoling Thoughts

14 Myths of the Widow's Grief

15 Only the Lonely Knows Its Pain

16 From Widows to Widows

17 Things Widows Should Know

18 The Grief That Does Not Speak

19 The Power of a Hug

20 Soak in the Promises

21 Getting to the Other Side of Grief

22 When You Need a Therapist

23 Anna's Counsel to Widows
24 Can Hardly Wait for Morning to Come
25 It's a New Relationship in Heaven
26 Clothed in a New Body
27 Where's Your Husband and What's He Doing
28 Good-byes Are Not Forever
29 Get Ready for the Reunion

Appendix One	Plan Ahead
Appendix Two	15 *Don't*s in Ministering to Widows
Appendix Three	10 Appropriate Things to Say to a Widow
Appendix Four	Resources for Widows
Appendix Five	Psalms for the Time of Grief

Endnotes

Preface

It's with a broken and bleeding heart you come to this book in a quest for support, guidance and healing in the aftermath of your husband's death. It's been my diligent and passionate effort in writing it not to disappoint. At the outset may I convey my deepest sympathy for the loss of life's most prized relationship, that with your loving husband.

As a widow you are now in the time of sorrow when the heart is ripped inside out; the time of crisis when you don't know where to turn; the time of rejection when some abandon you; the time of utter despondency when life hits the bottom; the time of disappointment when the heart is discouraged; the time of a new direction, when special guidance is needed; the time of questions and doubts when the heart searches for answers; the time of frustration when others just don't grasp the intense heart-wrenching pain and "lostness" you are bearing; and the time of desperation when you want to give up. The bottom line is that it's hard and painful without your husband here.

I realize that nothing that is written, even by the most astute, and certainly by me, will ever serve to minister totally to all those needs and heal the void created and pain experienced in your life and world by your husband's absence. Ultimately only God can do that or grant grace to live with it. But hopefully this small book may be found to grant some measure of comfort, peace, consolation, encouragement and hope as you seek relief, rest and recovery.

Words are the only tool at my disposal to minister to your deep hurt and wounds. And words in and of themselves cannot undo your sorrow. But they may help alleviate it and support you in it.

To that end this book has been written.

Help Other Grieving Widows Find Comfort
Other widows are hurting and grieving. You can help them by writing a concise review (two or three sentences) of *The Widow's Comfort* and posting it on the internet website where it was purchased. Your comments will encourage widows to get the book and thereby be benefited by it. If the book was given or acquired directly from the author, please email a review to frank@frankshivers.com. The few minutes it takes to submit a review could prove life-altering to others who are traveling the same journey of grief as you are.

Introduction

The grief of bereavement is the heaviest, most complicated and painful of all emotions. In order to know it, its despair, disorientation, helplessness, sorrow and challenges must be experienced firsthand. To survive it, it must be embraced personally and channeled properly. (Yes, that's easier said than done.)

"Widowhood is a desolate estate."[3] These words from the pen of Matthew Henry concisely describe the widow's extremity. When a husband dies, a wife's life is totally upended, thrusting her into an abyss of grief and heartache and change which she is ill-prepared to face. She meets bereavement without a navigation map and the necessary tools for its difficult journey. And she's lost, not knowing what to do, to whom to turn or what direction to go. Grief and mourning are the soundtrack of her life. It's on autoplay, playing continuously with musical notes that are piercing stabs of pain to the heart. Try as she will, she cannot stop the music—and she hides the torrent of tears it causes behind closed doors, while the world seems not to care, rushing on as if nothing has happened. (Grieving is exacerbated when it is largely ignored by others.)

And this crushes my heart.

She needs someone to care, to mend her broken heart, to stop the rain from falling down, to help her breathe again, to help her live again.

Despite my not being a psychologist, grief specialist or certified licensed counselor, and obviously not a widow who from experience knows the secrets of thwarting grief, the hurt of widows pressed me to undertake this writing to render any support possible, to mend their broken hearts and enable them to live again.

Within these pages may the widow find

(1 Life-giving answers to troublesome questions about the process of grief;

(2 Coping and healing medicines to relieve the intense pain, distress, loneliness, emptiness and worry spurred by grief;

(3 Resolution to religious doubts that grief has generated; and, ultimately,

(4 The peace of God that surpasses all understanding.

Throughout the book "healing" is not used to imply that grief is an illness to be "fixed," but that it is a trauma (broken heart) full of pain, sorrow, and discomfort (raw emotions) to be mended. Realization that in the early stages of grief attention span is short, the chapters have been kept brief, simple and pointed to enable quick review and application by the reader.

> To calm the sorrows of the mind,
>   Our heav'nly Friend is nigh,
> To wipe the anxious tear that starts
>   Or trembles in the eye.
>
> Thou canst, when anguish rends the heart,
>   The secret woe control;
> The inward malady canst heal,
>   The sickness of the soul.
>
> Thou canst repress the rising sigh,
>   Canst soothe each mortal care;
> And every deep and heartfelt groan
>   Is wafted to Thine ear.—Thomas Jervis (1812)

There are eleven million widows in America with one million new widows joining them every year. We must embrace them in our hearts, adopt them in our churches, support them with our gifts and envelope them in our prayers. To do more is warranted; to do less is unconscionable. It is this that Christ expects, solicits, requires, demands and judges.

Let us therefore hearken passionately and caringly to the task. "Take care of widows who are truly needy" (I Timothy 5:3 CEB). In so doing, we will be like Job, who said, "I caused the widow's heart to sing for joy" (29:13).

Oh, may our sympathizing breasts
    The generous pleasure know,
Kindly to share in others' joy
    And weep for others' woe!
—Philip Doddridge (1702–1751)

1   A Widow's Grief

"The death of a husband or wife is well recognized as an emotionally devastating event, being ranked on life-event scales as the most stressful of all possible losses."[4]
—Green, Solomon, and Osterweis

Jay Adams said, "Grief may be called a life-shaking sorrow over loss. Grief tears life to shreds; it shakes one from top to bottom. It pulls us loose. We come apart at the seams. Grief is nothing less than a life-shattering loss."[5]

What is a new widow's grief?

A widow's grief is a young widow raising her children alone. A widow's grief is the wife that frequents the cemetery to weep, remember and pray for consolation. A widow's grief is the empty chair at the table and missing body in the bed at night. A widow's grief is saying goodnight without hearing a response. A widow's grief is feeling she had been torn open and is bleeding from every part of her body. A widow's grief is hoping against hope that what happened is merely a bad dream, that she'll wake up and things will be back as they once were. A widow's grief is bitter loneliness and isolation. A widow's grief is numbness to that which she is experiencing. A widow's grief is the relentless tears that flow from her saddened eyes. A widow's grief is an internal dagger that injects its piercing blade into the heart a thousand times a day. A widow's grief is financial hardship. A widow's grief is desolation and agony. A widow's grief is emptiness and a hollowness. A widow's grief is at times camouflaged, giving the impression all is back to normal when it isn't and never will be. A widow's grief strikes fear in the heart about future uncertainties, paralyzing forward movement. A widow's grief is not having her actions and decisions understood. A widow's grief is loss of the rhythm and music of life. A widow's grief is a long, twisting, painful, difficult and seemingly unending journey accompanied by a cycle of varied emotions. A widow's grief is saying good-bye to the dreams of tomorrow with her husband stored in her heart. A widow's grief is struggling with when and how to say good-bye to her soulmate, lover, friend, provider and defender, and hello to a new form of existence without him. A widow's grief is that which is always an understatement to observers. A widow's grief is pushing forward a baby step at a time against the overwhelming internal desire not to "let go." A widow's grief is saying, "I'm okay," even when she's not okay. A widow's grief is being stereotyped as someone she is not. A widow's grief is having her prized possession become a buried treasure. A widow's grief is wanting to scream out of mere agony and heartbreak, but nothing comes out. A widow's grief is watching the life she expected vaporize in a matter of moments. A widow's grief is having a huge hole in the heart and universe that will never be filled. A widow's grief is moving on with life when she would rather not. A widow's grief is saying good-bye to the familiar, and hello to the strange, confusing, uncomfortable and frightful. A widow's grief is picking up the pieces and finding grace to press on with life when the other "half" of her has died.

George Wither, in "The Widow's Hymn," describes the anguish and sorrow of the widow.

How near me came the hand of Death,
    When at my side he struck my dear
And took away the precious breath
    Which quicken'd my beloved peer!
How helpless am I thereby made!
By day how grieved, by night how sad!
And now my life's delight is gone.
Alas! how am I left alone!— George Wither (1588–1667)

"What greater thing is there for two human souls than to feel that they are joined for life—to strengthen each other in all labor, to rest on each other in all sorrow, to minister to each other in all pain, to be one with each other in silent unspeakable memories at the moment of the last parting?"—George Eliot

2 The Widow's Care

"Prepare for a journey on the 'Sea of Nothingness.'"[6]
—Gerald Sittser

The Bible says (James 1:27), "Pure religion and undefiled before God and the Father is this, To visit…widows in their affliction." Believers are instructed to "visit" widows in times of trouble to render all manner of relief of which they are capable.[7] The duty, says James, defines the most genuine (spotless, pure) kind of faith and serves as a measuring standard of man's "religion." Despite the mandate, most churches don't have a program in place for their care. Neither are most believers sacrificially and compassionately making provision for them.

"Widows Indeed"

The kind of widows the church is to help are "widows indeed" (I Timothy 5:3). "Widows indeed" are those that are deserving of the church's support, having remained faithful to God and having cried out to Him "night and day" for help despite horrendous grief and trying circumstances (I Timothy 5:5). Her hope in the Lord is unwavering. Second, she is all alone without family support or care (I Timothy 5:4), and third, void of personal resources to care for herself. ("Not all widows are truly alone and without resources."[8]) The church (believers) should show "honor" ("to show respect," "to give assistance," or "treat graciously") to such widows by supplying all kinds of needs, but primarily financial support (Exodus 20:12; Deuteronomy 24:17; Matthew 15:1–6).

Obviously the church cannot give indiscriminately to every widow. Therefore, pastors and deacons ought to investigate every application by widows seeking help based upon biblical guidelines. This the early church did. J. Vernon McGee comments, "The early church took care of widows, but they didn't do it in some haphazard, sentimental way. The deacons were to make an investigation to see who were truly widows, where the need was, and how much need there was."[9] See Acts 6:1–6.

The Widow Needs

Manifold and numerous are the needs of widows that the church can supply (food, toiletries, money, prescriptions, clothes, yardwork, house repair or a gift that meets an immediate need). Transportation to church worship, events and activities, a need often overlooked, remains one of the most essential for many widows. Neglecting it multiplies their loneliness and despair, due to the loss of Christian fellowship. Caring for widows financially and otherwise communicates to them that they are loved and not alone.

Support from Family Primary and Pivotal

Widows, even the godliest, are to be supported by relatives, not the church (I Timothy 5:4, 8). Paul says that a widow's children and grandchildren have the obligation of requiting to her their gracious respect, caring attention, and financial provision. Larson writes, "Children and grandchildren have the opportunity to give back time, love and material support. They should also grow up with the expectation that this is their privilege and duty, especially to those widowed within their family. The church should be vocal and supportive in instilling these values in children and grandchildren."[10]

Rendering of such support by the widow's relatives allows the church to "care for the widows who are truly alone" (I Timothy 5:16 NLT). Matthew Henry said, "If any widow has children or nephews, that is grandchildren or near relations, let them maintain them, and let not the church be burdened."[11] John MacArthur states, "Caring for such a woman is a privilege and a manifestation of God's compassion. Paul said doing so 'is good and acceptable before God'. Parents deserve our respect and support, especially those who are widows."[12]

Many children live in luxury while their widowed mother lives in poverty, barely able to survive month to month. Failure to supply her need is despicable, disgraceful and an act of disobedience to the Lord, even if it is out of ignorance. Paul sternly states that a relative who fails to render care and support to the widowed in his family "has denied the faith and is worse than an unbeliever" (1 Timothy 5:8 NIV). What an indictment! The point? Genuine believers manifest benevolence and compassion to their widowed mother or grandmother.

Practical Acts of Kindness for the Widow

1. Provide and/or coordinate meals.
2. Run errands.
3. Maintain her auto.
4. Care for her lawn.
5. Provide transportation.
6. Help with groceries.
7. Lend a listening ear over a cup of coffee or luncheon.
8. Include her in social outings and hobbies.
9. Help with post-funeral estate matters.
10. Give financial assistance.

11. Instead of asking how you may help, suggest a way and do it with her permission.

12. Appropriate words of comfort, hope and concern spoken with sensitivity, compassion and wisdom at the right moment benefit the widow immensely. Solomon said a "word spoken in due season [a fitting word shared at the choicest of times], how good is it" (Proverbs 15:23). It's salving medicine to the broken heart.

13. Maintain connection with her beyond the funeral. It is needed more after it than before it.

14. Mark the calendar with the date of her husband's funeral as a reminder to reach out to her on that special day each year.

15. During special holidays (Thanksgiving, Christmas, New Years, Easter) the absence of her husband will be keenly felt. A card stating concern, support and prayers will be consoling and uplifting. E-cards are good, but physical cards are better.

Make Application for Assistance to the Church

As a "widow indeed" (true widow), you are biblically eligible for support from the body of Christ as deemed appropriate. God authorizes it. Scripture mandates it. The church supplies it (or should). Don't be hesitant, embarrassed or timid to request it.

3   Death, the Threshold to Something Better

"The proper epitaph to write for a Christian believer is not a dismal and uncertain petition, 'R.I.P.' ('may he rest in peace'), but a joyful and certain affirmation 'C.A.D.' ('Christ abolished death')."[13]—John W. Stott

Death seems senseless. It is named an enemy. It stops earthly pursuits and dreams. It is said to have a powerful stinger. It wounds, crushes and devastates lives. It attacks faith and hope. It ends earthly relationships (as it has yours). It refuses to be avoided. It creates void and emptiness in hearts. It afflicts with a pain that is almost unbearable. It seals from view what's beyond its door.

But Jesus says it's not without meaning and purpose, for it's the threshold that leads to life eternal in Heaven with Him and all the saints. So, what do we do when faced with the death of a loved one that crushes the heart and is beyond understanding? We remember that death possesses divine purpose and meaning for the Christian, the fullness of which cannot be fully comprehended or known at present. We remember that death is not a dead-end but a thoroughfare into the presence of Almighty God and the joys He has prepared for us in Heaven with our family and friends. We remember the words of Spurgeon: "Death to the saints is not a penalty; it is not destruction; it is not even a loss. It is a privilege.[14] It is the very joy of this earthly life to think that it will come to an end."[15]

And in remembering, we look death courageously in the face and say with Paul, "O death, where is thy sting [pain]? O grave, where is thy victory [power]? The sting of death is sin; and the strength of sin is the law. But thanks be to God, which giveth us the victory through our Lord Jesus Christ" (1 Corinthians 15:55–57).

Max Lucado provides inspirational insight. "In God's plan every life is long enough and every death is timely. And although you and I might wish for a longer life, God knows better. And—this is important—although you and I may wish a longer life for our loved ones, they don't. Ironically, the first to accept God's decision of death is the one who dies. While we are shaking heads in disbelief, they are lifting hands in worship. While we are mourning at a grave, they are marveling at Heaven. While we are questioning God, they are praising God."[16]

"Death is the last and best physician," states Thomas Watson, "which cures all diseases and sins—the aching head and the unbelieving heart. Sin was the midwife which brought death into the world, and death shall be the grave to bury sin! Oh, the privilege of a believer!"[17] Saith John MacArthur in agreement, "Death is not a sad event; death is a joyous event because this is what ushers us into that which God has prepared for us to enjoy forever."[18] See John 11:25.

> *Death is not a sad event; death is a joyous event because this is what ushers us into that which God has prepared for us to enjoy forever. —John MacArthur*

4   Grieving Isn't Craziness

"I not only live each endless day in grief, but live each day thinking about living each day in grief."[19]
—C. S. Lewis

You're not crazy, gone mad or "out of your head" to intensely grieve. However, its painful symptoms that fuel irrational thinking and decisions may make you think that you're going crazy. That's normal, healthy and expected. It goes with the territory. You don't need psychiatric treatment.

Paul sanctioned grief over death, provided we "sorrow not, even as others which have no hope" (1 Thessalonians

4:13). "Human sorrow," states John MacArthur, "is a natural emotion [not a mental disease]. Our Lord Himself was 'a man of sorrows, and acquainted with grief' (Isaiah 53:3). It is a God-given relief valve for the pain and sorrow in this fallen world and promotes the healing process."[20] "There may be sorrow, there must be sorrow, under the afflictions and bereavements of life; only it should not be despondent sorrow, nor rebellious sorrow, nor murmuring sorrow, but sorrow submissive and sanctifying."[21]

Benefits of grief

Grieving much and deeply manifests tremendous love.

Grief is relieved by grieving (internal emotions of sorrow) and mourning (eternal expressions of sorrow).

Grief is a good teacher that instructs you how to help others that grieve.

With grief comes empathy for other grievers.

Grief deepens trust in and dependence upon God.

Grief reminds us of the transitoriness of life.

Grief bolsters confidence in the ability to cope successfully with life's hardest trials. Vance Havner, a few days after his wife's death, wrote: "There is not much that I dread from here on out. When one has drained the bitterest cup, he is better prepared for any other potion that life may serve."[22]

Grief unites families and friends with a deeper bond.

Grief enables you to reach a point where you can "breathe again," live with your loss in a healthy way.

Grief gradually enables adjustment to a continuing but "new" relationship with your husband.

Grief spurs internal (spiritual and emotional) and external (physical and social) changes necessary to a holistic (comprehensive well-being) outlook and state.

Although it's difficult today
    To see beyond the sorrow,
May looking back in memory
    Help comfort you tomorrow.—Author Unknown

"Respond in grief," advises Jim Henry, "until you find relief. If we bury our grief, it is like toxic waste. It will surface again, and the contamination makes for more trouble."[23]

Types of Grief

Normal Grief—Marked movement toward resolution of grief

Anticipatory Grief—Grief prior to the loss of a loved one

Chronic Grief—Extreme distress without progress in its subsiding

Delayed Grief—Suppression of grief to a time long after the funeral

Distorted Grief—Atypical reactions to death

Cumulative Grief—When one death is soon followed by another

Absent Grief—Denial of the death of the loved one

Exaggerated Grief—Intensification of normal grief reactions that may worsen

Isolated Grief—Grief borne alone

5   Coping with Your Feelings

"The reality is that you will grieve forever. You will not get over the loss of a loved one; you'll learn to live with it. You will be whole again, but you will never be the same."[24]—Elisabeth Kubler-Ross

Emotions of Grief That Widows May Experience

Shock. Initially, a numbing paralysis. Takes time for the emotions to assimilate what happened.

Denial or disbelief. "This has to be a dream. It didn't really happen."

Sorrow. Mixture of despair, longing, regret and sadness.

Depression. Feelings of hopelessness and helplessness that result in grave despondency.

Fear. C. S. Lewis, following the death of his wife, said, "No one ever told me that grief felt so like fear."[25] Grief feels like fear because it is shrouded with uncertainties.

Emptiness and loneliness. The absence of your husband has created a hole in your heart that nothing can fill, causing a feeling of aloneness.

Memories. Memories is the house where your husband now lives. Visiting it evokes intense pain for some, while others attest to its healing and comfort.

Disorientation. Fogginess regarding life and its responsibilities.

Deprivation. Food, sleep and/or hygiene are neglected or rejected.

Withdrawal. Seclusion from life socially and inattentiveness to its duties and obligations.

Guilt. "If only I had done more or gotten him a better doctor."

Anger. Related to "fight, flight or freeze" over the "unfairness" of facing life without your soulmate.

Acceptance. To heal you must embrace the reality of the death of your husband (not the notion of being "all right" with it; that will never happen). Michael Kreal says, "Our dislike of saying that someone is dead reveals the profoundness of our death denials."[26]

Ten Facts about Emotions of Grief

Fact #1

Sorrow is not forbidden by God. Saith F. B. Meyer, "Scripture never condemns grief [emotions of sorrow]."[27] Neither is it optional. All must embrace it. It is a normal and healthy response to the loss of someone you loved. The only biblical prohibition to sorrow is that it be not like that of the unbeliever (without hope of life beyond the grave with Christ in Heaven—1 Thessalonians 4:13).

"Tears are a tribute," saith Matthew Henry, "to our deceased friends. When the body is sown, it must be watered. But we must not sorrow as those that have no hope; for we have a good hope through grace both concerning them and concerning ourselves."[28]

Helen Founleson, Scottish martyr executed at Perth in 1544, illustrates the believer's hope. Being refused the request to die with her husband, she kissed him at the very gallows on which he was to be executed saying, "Husband, rejoice, for we have lived together many joyful days, but this day, in which we must die, ought to be the most joyful to us both, because we must have joy forever. Therefore, I will not bid you good-night, for we shall suddenly meet with joy in the kingdom of Heaven."[29]

Fact #2

"You can't see anything properly while your eyes are blurred with tears," says C. S. Lewis.[30] Grief all too often is blind to time, truth, reality and God's plan. Walk by faith, not by feelings. Grief pines for reunion immediately, not in months or years. It speaks of an exodus from life to be with your husband—NOW. Consoling it is to know that the Apostle Paul longed to be with the Lord but refused to hurry it along. He says, "To me, living means having Christ. To die means that I would have more of Him. If I keep on living here in this body, it means that I can lead more people to Christ" (Philippians 1:21–22 NLV). Though desirous to be with the Lord immediately, he realized God's purpose for his life had not been finished. May solace in the dilemma regarding your husband (be with him now or continue with life) be found in these words.

Fact #3

No model of grief exists that fits all. Each widow has her own unique journey of grief which is shaped by complex emotions (acknowledged and unacknowledged), memories and stimuli.[31] No two widows walk the *same path* of grief in its disparagement, difficulty, duration and dissolution.

Fact #4

While the scope of things that accompany grief are in general predictable, *they are not applicable to all*. For example, one widow may experience denial regarding her husband's death, whereas another accepts it from the start.

Fact #5

There is no fast, ironclad rule on having to walk through certain stages or phases of grief, despite various suppositions that grief has a set pattern. A widow may experience only one stage of grief, skipping all the others.

It's the widow, not the psychologist that "wrote the book" on the stages of grief, who determines her grief experience. C. H. Spurgeon well says, "Sorrow is not a stage you get through, but rather a process you live with."[32]

Fact #6

It is noteworthy that the stages of grief (various emotions or feelings) may not occur sequentially or only once. A widow may experience one, then another, only then to regress back to the first.[33] Two stages of grief may occur simultaneously.

Fact #7

The grief of the widow is based on her love for her husband and its magnitude. To have loved deeply is to grieve profoundly. The more closely attached we are to others, the greater the grief in the aftermath of their death (the severing or ripping apart of that strong attachment). Don't judge the rightness of your grief journey based upon that of another widow.

Fact #8

Grieving (internal emotions of sorrow) and mourning (outward expressions or signs of grief like crying, journaling, talking about the grief, etc.) are essential to the healing process. Don't attempt to escape or skip the pain and distress. Samuel Johnson said, "While grief is fresh, every attempt to divert only irritates. You must wait till it be digested."[34] Chuck Swindoll concurs, saying, "You can't resolve the pain by changing your circumstances or running away. Grief is a journey that you must go through, one day at a time."[35]

Grief has to work its way through whatever stages or passages that are expedient and necessary for healing. Don't shortchange it. To grieve internally, to express it externally (mourning), is to heal.

Fact #9

Although grief will lessen, it never totally dissipates. "The good news," states Spurgeon, "is that, by God's grace, in time the sorrowing sadness will lessen more and more, giving way to sweet sadness."[36] The crushing hurt won't last forever. Trust God's promise: "He brought them out of their gloom and darkness and broke their chains in pieces" (Psalm 107:14 GNT).

Fact #10

Signs of 'complicated grief' include a *persistent* extreme focus on and pining for your husband, difficulty accepting his death, feeling of meaninglessness, intense sorrow and the inability to enjoy life.

"Suffering has been stronger than all other teaching and has taught me to understand what your heart used to be."[37]
—Charles Dickens

6   Basic Essentials for Healing

"I know well there is no comfort for this pain of parting. The wound always remains, but one learns to bear the pain and learns to thank God for what He gave, for the beautiful memories of the past and the yet more beautiful hope for the future."[38]—Max Müller

While each widow experiences a grief uniquely different from that of others, they share seven basic needs for healing (coping successfully with the deaths of their husbands). The timeframe and sequence for accomplishing this vary from widow to widow. There is no set governing rule.

1) Acknowledgement of death's reality. Grief is what you experience internally following the death of your husband. In a place of solitude ponder your inner thoughts and feelings about his death. Look grief in the face and

bravely say hello to it.[39] Saying hello to death's reality continues by mourning.

2) Saying good-bye to your husband. By saying hello to the loss of your husband and to grief, mourning and change, with the help of the Holy Spirit and the support of the saints, in time you will be able to say a kind of good-bye. You don't get over his death or forget it, but become reconciled to it.[40] "Saying good-bye," says Alan D. Wolfelt, "is not the same as 'closure.' You never fully close the door on the love and grief you feel for someone who has died. But you can achieve a sense of peace. The days of intense and constant turmoil can be replaced by serene acceptance as well as days of love, hope and joy."[41]

3) Venting of pent-up emotions. Suppressed emotions cause serious medical issues. Look for avenues to release them. *Crying.* Dr. Karl Menninger states, "Weeping is perhaps the most human and universal of all relief measures."[42] "There is a sacredness in tears," states Washington Irving. "They are not the mark of weakness, but of power. They speak more eloquently than ten thousand tongues. They are the messengers of overwhelming grief, of deep contrition, and of unspeakable love."[43] It's always okay to cry. It's like the release valve on a pressure cooker. It keeps the heart from exploding. *Praying.* Chuck Swindoll counsels, "Tell God what's in your heart. Let it out and don't hold back. He can handle it."[44] John Flavel wrote, "That which begins not with prayer, seldom winds up with comfort."[45] *Sharing.* Mal and Dianne McKissock state, "One of the greatest needs of all bereaved people is to have access to someone who will take a risk and be involved—someone who is not afraid of intense feelings, but who will encourage their expression, confident that this is part of the 'healing' process."[46] *Journaling.* Express your deepest emotions with pen and paper.

4) Letting go of the "Why" question. Although asking "why" ("why his death and not mine") is natural, it cannot be answered to our satisfaction and serves only to intensify and prolong mourning. There can be no healing for mourning and grief until the "why" is placed in trust in God's hands to be revealed in eternity where then it will make sense. The question to ask is not "Why," but "How?" How can I have courage and strength to continue to live and serve the Lord despite his absence? See Chapter 8: "Dark Yesterdays and Todays Become Bright Tomorrows."

5) Keeping the memories alive. Memories are the glue that helps keep your life from falling apart into multiple irreparable broken pieces. Don't suppress memories of your husband nor allow others to pressure you to stifle them. Your husband, although absent, is yet with you through memories. See chapter 11: "Healing Through Memories."

6) Conceding that you are now on a new path. One life has been lost; you must now remake another. Robert Neimeyer wrote, "Grieving individuals can be viewed as struggling to affirm or reconstruct a personal world of meaning that has been challenged by loss."[47] Plans and dreams were crushed the moment your husband died—and with them life's meaning and purpose. With God's guidance, set a new course with new plans, dreams and aspirations. Rebuild a relationship with the world. Though life will never be as marvelous and happy as it was with your husband in it, it can yet be wonderful and joyous. "When we lose someone we love, we must learn not to live without them, but to live with the love they left behind."[48]

7) Leaning on others for support. Avoid withdrawal and isolation. Find ways to get out of the house. Phillip Yancy cautions, "Do not attempt healing alone. The real healing of deep connective tissue takes place in community. Where is God when it hurts? Where God's people are. Where misery is, there is the Messiah; and on

this earth, the Messiah takes form in the shape of His church. That's what the body of Christ means."[49] As with the widow Anna (Luke 2) you will find repose, renewal and restoration in the fellowship with the saints (see chapter 23).

Billy Graham said, "Grief that is not dealt with properly can cause us to lose our perspective on life."[50] "Grieving properly," states J. I. Packer, "leads back to thinking properly, living properly and praising properly. God sees to that!"[51]

"They shall be comforted" (Matthew 5:4). R. May writes, "This intimates certainty as well as the futurity of the comfort. But some may ask: 1. What is this consolation? It arises from the satisfaction Christ has made—none so rich, free and satisfying as this. 2. Whence does this comfort proceed? From the free favor of God. 3. How is this comfort applied? It is the work of the Holy Spirit."[52]

7 Moving On Is Not Forgetting or Betraying Him

"If there ever comes a day when we can't be together, keep me in your heart. I'll stay there forever."[53]—A. A. Milne, Winnie the Pooh

Piecing together the shattered emotions and broken pieces of your heart is not forgetting or betraying your husband. Moving forward is not saying you are over his death. That will never happen. Elisabeth Kubler-Ross and David Kessler said, "The reality is that you will grieve forever. You will not 'get over' the loss of a loved one; you'll learn to live with it. You will heal and you will rebuild yourself around the loss you have suffered. You will be whole again, but you will never be the same. Nor should you be the same, nor would you want to."[54]

The diminishing of grief with its despair and the enjoying of life again doesn't equate with missing your husband any less. It will not cause a "break" in contact or loss of connection with him. What it will do is free you to honor him by living life to the fullest by not pining obsessively and relentlessly over that which cannot be changed. Remember, it's not in your pain from grief that his memory lives and survives, but in YOU.[55] The absence of deep pain and anguish will not injure his memory or your connection to him one iota. Grasp the fact that the diminishing pain does not mean your husband is disappearing; you're just learning how to live with his memory differently.[56]

15 Ways to Stay Connected to Your Husband

"Keep me near you like a seal you wear over your heart, like a signet ring you wear on your hand. Love is as strong as death" (Song of Solomon 8:6 ERV). Use whatever appropriate means of remembrance that promote healing for you and connection to your husband. They in turn will gradually replace the pain without eliciting fear that you are letting go of him.[57] Havelock Ellis said, "All the art of living lies in a fine mingling of letting go and holding on."[58]

1. *Continuation of his life's ambition and work.* Susannah Spurgeon kept publishing her husband's (Charles') books and distributed them freely. Elizabeth Elliot maintained the mission work of her husband (Jim).

2. *Scholarship funding and endowments to the field of his passion.*

3. *Acts of service in tribute to his life.*

4. *Gifting money in his name to further causes that he supported.*

5. *Incorporation into your life of one or more disciplines he embraced.*

6. *Involvement in the church that he attended.*

7. *Maintaining connection with his family and closest friends.*

8. *Keeping alive that which was important to him.*

9. *A linking object that connects you with him and evokes happiness.*[59] David M. Reiss states, "A linking object should be a comforting aid that can be called on at certain times, but not the object of obsession or rigid ritual."[60]

10. *Celebrate his birthday.*

11. *Develop a memory treasure chest* (photos, letters, etc.).

12. *Wearing of a necklace with his wedding band attached.*

13. *Saved emails, phone text and voice messages from him.*

14. *Listening to his speeches, sermons, songs.*

15. *Occasional visits to the cemetery.*

"Thou shalt be missed, because thy seat will be empty" (I Samuel 20:18). These words of Jonathan to David ring true about your husband. With his favorite chair vacant in your home, he is sorely missed. However, though empty, it's not silent, for it still speaks for him (from an inexhaustible bank of memories), providing comfort, love, hope and encouragement.

"When the sun finally drops below the horizon in the early evening, evidence of its work remains for some time. The skies continue to glow for a full hour after its departure. In the same way, when a good or a great person's life comes to its final sunset, the skies of this world are illuminated until long after he is out of view. Such a person does not die from this world, for when he departs, he leaves much of himself behind—and being dead, he still speaks."[61]

Look beyond the empty chair
    To know a life well spent;
Look beyond the solitude
    To days of true content.

Cherish in your broken heart
    Each moment gladly shared
And feel the touch of memory
    Beyond the empty chair.—Catherine Turner

> You are near, even if I don't see you. You are with me, even if you are far away. You are in my heart, in my thoughts, in my life...always.

Your husband, although moved away, has not dropped out of your life. He remains with you in a thousand ways. For a truth you may say of him, "You are near, even if I don't see you. You are with me, even if you are far away. You are in my heart, in my thoughts, in my life...always."[62]

8   Dark Yesterdays and Todays Become Bright Tomorrows

"Were it not for the consciousness of Christ in my life, hour by hour, I could not go on. But He is teaching me the glorious lessons of His sufficiency, and each day I am carried onward with no feeling of strain or fear of collapse."[63]—Hudson Taylor

You don't need empty platitudes and religious jargon, preacherish clichés and "standardized" condolences, or explanations and speculations. Billy Graham states, "If there is something we need more than anything else during grief, it is a friend who stands with us, who doesn't leave us. Jesus is that friend."[64] Joseph Stowell agrees, stating, "Even though your heart is breaking and tears are clouding your eyes and staining your cheeks, God does give us something worth trusting in tough times—and that's Him, and Him alone."[65] John W. Stott said, "Stronger than any chemical tranquilizer is trust in our all-knowing God."[66]

The Holy Scripture provides ample reason for every widow to exhibit uninhibited trust (faith) in the Lord with every care. He is their *refuge* in the time of trouble and tribulation (Psalm 46:1–2); *strong tower* in the time of personal conflict (Psalm 61:3); *strong Rock* in times of weakness and frailty (Psalm 31:2); that *friend that sticketh closer than a brother* in times of horrendous grief, sorrow and loneliness (Proverbs 18:24); *the potter* who takes the broken pieces of one's life and molds them into something beautiful (Isaiah 64:8); *the vine* supplying nutrition to the branches (His children) that they may experience abundant life and bear much fruit for the kingdom of God (John 15:5); *the wonderful counsellor* to impart wisdom for handling life's problems and pains (Isaiah 9:6; John 14:16); *the Good Shepherd* that lays down His life for His sheep that they might be saved and secured (John 10:11); *the light of the world* illuminating the spiritual darkness, showing man the right path to travel (John 8:12); *the great emancipator* setting the prisoner free from the strongholds of satanic bondage (John 8:36); *the bread of life* that satisfies the longing of the soul (John 6:35–51); and *the sympathizing Jesus* who "speaks the drooping heart to cheer."[67] The psalmist says, 'The Lord sustains [*"relieves, restores, raises up from their low condition"*[68]]...the widow' (Psalm 146:9).

John Ortberg says, "There is something you can't fix, can't heal or can't escape; and all you can do is trust God. Finding *ultimate refuge* in God means you become so immersed in His presence, so convinced of His goodness, so devoted to His lordship, that you find even the cave is a perfectly safe place to be because He is there with you."[69] Knowing He is there with you, even in this "there" of grief and sorrow, instills calm, comfort and courage.

When nothing whereon to lean remains,
    When strongholds crumble to dust,
When nothing is sure but that God still reigns,
    That is just the time to trust.[70] —John Oxenham

The psalmist said, "God is our refuge and strength, a very present help in trouble. Therefore will not we fear" (Psalm 46:1–2). He that trusts Him wholly finds Him wholly able to render the assistance needed. Alexander Maclaren says, "Trust [God] as what He is, and trust Him because of what He is, and see to it that your faith lays hold on the living God Himself and on nothing besides."[71]

Although there are no easy answers or glib spiritual maxims to "fix" your grief immediately, trust God's ableness and willingness (promises) to transform the dark yesterdays and todays into bright tomorrows.[72]

9 Alligators and Grief

"In the dark night, my prayers feel like they reach no higher than the ceiling. In the dark night, the Bible I read turns to ashes. In the dark night, words and books and songs that once spoke to my soul now leave me cold."[73]
—John Ortberg

A small boy went for a swim in the old swimming hole behind his home. Unknown to him as he swam toward the middle of the lake, an alligator was swimming toward him. The watchful eye of his father saw what was transpiring, and he quickly ran to the water, shouting the danger to his son. The lad made a U-turn to swim to him. Reaching from the dock, the father grabbed his son's arms just as the alligator snatched his legs. An incredible tug-of-war raged. Battling a strength greater than his own, the father would not let go. A farmer passing by in his truck heard the screams, raced to the water and shot the alligator. Miraculously, following weeks of hospitalization, the young boy recovered. The severe scars on his legs bore witness to the traumatizing and almost fatal encounter with the alligator, while the deep scratches on his arms showed the marks of his father's fingernails that dug into his flesh to hang on to him. A reporter asked to see the scars. The boy pulled up his pant legs. And then the boy said, "But look at my arms. I have great scars on my arms, too, because my dad wouldn't let go."

Regardless of the *alligators* (grief, fear, loneliness, worry, etc.) that afflict and assail you, bringing hurt and pain, the heavenly Father will not let go of you—even when you want to let go, like Elijah (1 Kings 19:4) and Jonah (Jonah 4:3) did.

The scars in His hands, feet and side bear indisputable testimony to that. God securely grips your hand in this storm of grief, refusing to let go. He says, "That's right. Because I, your GOD, have a firm grip on you and I'm not letting go. I'm telling you, 'Don't panic. I'm right here to help you'" (Isaiah 41:13 MSG). Your grip on Him may waver, but not His upon you. Knowing He holds your hand tightly and firmly, what have you to dread or fear from the "alligators"?

Jesus will walk with me, guarding me ever,
  Giving me victory thru storm and thru strife;
He is my Comforter, Counselor, Leader
  Over the uneven journey of life.—Haldor Lillenas (1922)

10   Not a Tear Goes Unnoticed

"Tears are the noble language of eyes, and when true love of words is destitute. The eye by tears speak, while the tongue is mute."[74]—Robert Herrick

    It's OKAY to cry. Dickens said, "We need never be ashamed of our tears."[75] Tears are unspeakable words that must be spoken. Saith F. B. Meyer, "Tears are valuable. They are God-given relief mechanisms. Tears discharge the insupportable agony of the heart, as an overflow lessens the pressure of the flood against the dam."[76] Thomas Paine said, "Tears may soothe the wounds they cannot heal."[77] Therefore, when tears swell in the eyes and you fight to restrain them, ponder Mr. Bumbles' line from Charles Dickens' *Oliver Twist*: "It opens the lungs, washes the countenance, exercises the eyes, and softens down the temper. So, cry away!"[78] "Tears are agony in solution."[79] They are healing in action, one teardrop at a time.

    Not a tear in the vast ocean of tears that have been shed is unnoticed by God. David said, "The LORD hath heard the voice of my weeping" (Psalm 6:8). God says to all what He said to Hezekiah, "I have seen thy tears" (2 Kings 20:5). The psalmist says, "You've [God] kept track of my every toss and turn through the sleepless nights, each tear entered in your ledger [and bottle], each ache written in your book" (Psalm 56:8 MSG). Chuck Swindoll states, "A teardrop on earth summons the King of Heaven. Rather than being ashamed or disappointed, the Lord takes note of our inner friction when hard times are oiled by tears. He turns these situations into moments of tenderness; He never forgets those crises in our lives where tears were shed."[80] What consolation to know that God sees, saves and understands every teardrop that falls from your eyes.

But a day is coming when "the voice of weeping shall be no more heard" (Isaiah 65:19). Spurgeon comments about that wondrous day: "The glorified weep no more, for all outward causes of grief are gone. No pain distresses; no thought of death or bereavement saddens. They dwell within a city which shall never be stormed; they bask in a sun which shall never set; they drink of a river which shall never dry; they pluck fruit from a tree which shall never wither."[81] Heaven is a place where "God will take away all their tears. There will be no more death or sorrow or crying or pain. All the old things have passed away" (Revelation 21:4 NLV). It is an abode where painful sorrow and suffering are eternally banished. Hallelujah!

The Bible says that God presently "healeth the broken in heart, and bindeth up their wounds" (Psalm 147:3). God is always ready to take His handkerchief of love and tenderness and wipe the tears from the face of His child, giving consolation and comfort. This He has done faithfully and compassionately to the extent that an Ocean of Tears can be formed from them. And that which He has done for others, He stands ready to do for you—right now! Just ask Him.

11   Healing through Memories

"Each day is a gift, and as long as my eyes open,
I'll focus on the new day and all the happy memories
I've stored away, just for this time in my life."[82]— Unknown

What is the continuing relationship with your husband NOW? It is that of memories that speak of the cherished relationship. They are the primary way to sustain the relationship.[83] "Memory is the treasure house of the mind," says Thomas Fuller, "wherein the monuments [of your husband] thereof are kept and preserved."[84] And the memories possess emotional, medicinal and comforting value. Allison Gilbert says, "The prescription for joy and healing after loss is to remember."[85] There's a school of thought that disagrees with her, that says the widow should shun memories, especially when grief is raw and fresh. The memories would be too painful. But the opposite is actually the case, at least for most.[86] (For those to whom they are painful, a shift will occur in time when their bittersweetness will turn to all delight.)

> "I will hold you in my heart, until I can hold you again in heaven."—Unknown

The joy of remembering helps ease the pain of the heart-wrenching loss of your husband in five ways. Memories help fill the painful void of your husband's absence. Memories remind you of an enduring and indissoluble bond with him. Memories galvanize and invigorate the relationship. Memories replace the despair of missing him, even if initially only momentarily, with joyance. Memories remind you of the joy, smiles and laughter he showered upon you and brought into your life, lifting your spirit. Therefore, stoke the fire of remembrance of your husband and be benefited thereby (profited) emotionally. Permit the memories. Prompt them. Ponder them. Proclaim them. Preserve them.

Meik Wiking, a researcher at the Happiness Research Institute, agrees with my assessment. He states, "Happy memories form the cornerstone of our identity and can help with combating depression and loneliness. They influence our happiness in the current moment, as well as providing a framework for our hopes and dreams about the future."[87] "Remembering and sharing the past," writes Alan D. Wolfelt, "makes hoping for the future possible. Your future will become open to new experiences only to the extent that you embrace the past."[88]

> *God gave us memories that we might have roses in December.— J. M. Barrie*

J. M. Barrie said, "God gave us memories that we might have roses in December."[89] Corrie ten Boom stated, "Memories are the key not to the past, but to the future."[90] An unknown author said, "When someone you love becomes a memory, the memory becomes a treasure." "Photos can capture our memories in print," says Catherine Pulsifer, "but our memories are always with us in our minds."[91]

Precious memories, how they linger;
   How they ever flood my soul!
In the stillness of the midnight,
   Precious sacred scenes unfold.
   Precious memories fill my soul.—J. B. F. Wright (1877)

Remembrance, the Lasting Perfume

Saith the poet Jean de Boufflers, "Pleasure is the flower that passes; remembrance, the lasting perfume."[92] The perfume (memories) is packaged in photographs, memorabilia, a playlist of his favorite songs, souvenirs, scrapbooks, letters, conversations, storytelling, DVDs and videos, and thoughts. Smell it often. It provides healing, health and happiness.

"In the garden of memory, in the palace of dreams…that is where you and I shall meet."[93] — Lewis Carroll

12 Bethany Is No Longer Bethany

Oh, for the touch of a vanished hand and the sound of a voice that is still![94]—Alfred Tennyson

"Jesus wept"—not for Lazarus but for the breakup of the Bethany home; it would never be the same.[95] (He wept in compassion for Mary and Martha, Lazarus' sisters.) And this is the element of death that makes it sadder and more grievous. Bethany is no longer Bethany because the chair of your husband is empty.

And it never will be the old Bethany again. It's not what you want. You want it like it was before, but the harsh reality is that your life has changed, and there is nothing that can be done to alter that fact.

But with this anomaly, the Lord will step by step give grace to adapt to a new normal. Adjustment to a life without your husband happens in bits and pieces. Baby steps in time will turn into big ones. Day by day and moment by moment you will gain strength to adjust to the new you and new path.

Some days it may feel that two steps were taken backwards. Other days huge strides are experienced. The secret is not to give up, to keep pressing forward however uncomfortable and difficult the change, not to resist it—and remember. "Sometimes people around you won't understand your journey. They don't need to; it's not for them."[96]

13   Consoling Thoughts

"Hope is one of the Theological virtues. This means that a continual looking forward to the eternal world is not (as some modern people think) a form of escapism or wishful thinking, but one of the things a Christian is meant to do."[97]—C. S. Lewis

"May there be such a oneness between us that your tears flow down my cheeks."—Frank Shivers

"Death leaves a heartache no one can heal; love leaves a memory no one can steal."—From an Irish headstone

"For each thorn, there's a rosebud…
    For each twilight, a dawn…
For each trial, the strength
    To carry on.
For each storm cloud, a rainbow…
    For each shadow, the sun…
For each parting, sweet memories
    When sorrow is done."[98]—Ralph Waldo Emerson

"To ease another's heartache is to forget one's own."[99]—Abraham Lincoln

"Gone some few, trifling steps ahead
   And nearer to the end,
So that you, too,
   Once past the bend,
Shall meet again,
   As face to face, this friend."[100]—Robert Louis Stevenson

"Loving someone changes us forever. So does losing them."[101]—Alan D. Wolfelt

"Relying on God has to begin all over again every day, as nothing has yet been done."[102]—C. S. Lewis

"Our hope must be built on Christ alone and on the promises God has given us in His Word."[103]—Billy Graham

"We hear tears loudly on this side of Heaven. What we don't take time to contemplate are the even louder cheers on the other side of death's valley."[104]—Zig Ziglar

"What we once enjoyed and deeply loved we can never lose, for all that we love deeply becomes a part of us."[105]—Helen Keller

"The grave is but the threshold of eternity. What a world were this, how unendurable its weight, if they whom death hath sundered, did not meet again!"[106]—Robert Southey

"We see His smile of love even when others see nothing but the black hand of Death smiting our best beloved."[107]—C. H. Spurgeon

"The pain of grief is just as much part of life as the joy of love. It is perhaps the price we pay for love, the cost of commitment."[108]—Colin Parkes

"We've shared our lives these many years. You've held my hand; you've held my heart. So many blessings, so few tears—yet for a moment, we must part."—Unknown

"Grief expected, but it is different from the grief of the world. There is a difference between tears of hope and tears of hopelessness."[109]—Erwin Lutzer

"It's so much darker when a light goes out than it would have been if it had never shone."[110]—John Steinbeck

"O thou afflicted, tossed with tempest and not comforted, this alone can give thee calm when the storms of life beat wildly and the waves run high, to know that thy life is being lived within the sheltering care of God."[111]—Henry Howard

"There are some who bring a light so great to the world that even after they have gone the light remains."—Unknown

"Bereavement is not the truncation of married love but one of its regular phases—like the honeymoon. What we want is to live our marriage well and faithfully through that phase too."[112]—C. S. Lewis

"When one tries to recapture that which is gone forever, it brings frustration and sometimes depression."[113]—Billy Graham

"If it were possible to heal sorrow by weeping and to raise the dead with tears, gold were less prized than grief."[114]—Sophocles

14 Myths of the Widow's Grief

"The irony of grief is that the person you most want to talk to about it is no longer here."—Anonymous

MYTH: Pain dissipates faster when we ignore it.

Fact: Ignoring or stifling the pain that resulted in the death of your husband only makes it fester and grow worse.

MYTH: It's important to put on a strong face before your children.

Fact: Don't cover up that which is natural and expected (fear, hurt, confusion, loneliness, etc.). You need not try to protect your children from seeing your pain. It will be beneficial to them.

MYTH: If you don't cry, you're not really sorry over your husband's death.

Fact: Crying, though a normal response to loss, is not the only one. Other ways of expressing grief are just as real and genuine.

MYTH: The duration for grief is about a year.

Fact: The process of grief is unique to each widow. There is no right or wrong time frame. Chuck Swindoll said, "The grieving process can't be hurried. It takes time."[115] There's no reward for hurriedness.

MYTH: Time heals grief.

Fact: Time alone doesn't heal the broken heart. Grieving over time helps heal it. "You don't heal," states Carol Crandall, "from the loss of a loved one because time passes you; you heal because of what you do with the time."[116] As time itself cannot inflate a flat tire, so it cannot mend a broken heart. Without decisive action—the implementation of healing agents—there is no healing.

MYTH: Where faith is strong, grief won't be long.

Fact: Grief's duration is not an indicator of the degree of faith. Chuck Swindoll said, "The length of a person's recovery says nothing about his or her spirituality. The mourning process is just as individual and unique as a fingerprint."[117]

MYTH: By overcoming grief I will dishonor my husband.

Fact: In truth, by diminishing grief you will actually honor him by moving on with life and God's plan. To move ahead may feel like abandonment of him. But's it's not. That will never happen. Therefore, reject that lie that Satan seeks to sow in your thoughts.

MYTH: Talking about grief only makes it worse.

Fact: Refusal to articulate your grief traps its pain inside. Talking about it frees it. Christie Eastman, a Certified Emotionally Focused Therapist, says, "Grief that is unaddressed, put aside, numbed, stuffed down, or shut off can grow bigger and less manageable."[118]

MYTH: Grief has an end point.

Fact: Although the intensity and form of grief changes, it never ends.

MYTH: It's time to let go of my grief and move on with my life, my friends say.

Fact: The clock of grief ticks according to the person. It cannot be sped up. That which may be the experience of another is not applicable to you.

MYTH: Healing of grief means you have gotten over the death of your husband.

Fact: The truth is that although you will learn to cope better with his absence, you never will get over his death.

MYTH: Grief is a sign of weak faith.

Fact: Billy Graham says, "When we grieve over someone who has died in Christ, we are sorrowing not for them but for ourselves. Our grief isn't a sign of weak faith, but of great love."[119]

MYTH: If I'm not crying, something is wrong with me.

Fact: Everyone grieves differently. The absence of tears does not indicate that a widow's grief is less horrendous than that of another.

MYTH: Bereavement often requires psychiatric or medicinal treatment.

Fact: Grieving and mourning are normal. Therefore, as a rule, medical or psychological intervention is unnecessary.

MYTH: There are set stages of grief that all widows must experience for healing.

Fact: Grief is unpredictable and impacts each widow differently. C. S. Lewis said in the aftermath of his wife's death, "I thought I could describe a state, make a map of sorrow. Sorrow, however, turns out to be not a state but a process."[120] Grief is an unpredictable journey, not a set of definitive steps or stages. The bereaved are often misguided by teachings that say they will experience this stage and that stage in the grief process. "Staging" persons who are coping with death need to stop.

MYTH: Grief is not a full-body experience.

Fact: As grief affects mental health, it also impacts the body physiologically (body aches and pains, heart issues, blood pressure elevation, headaches, fatigue, digestive complications, sleep disturbance, rapid heartbeat, etc.[121]).

15   Only the Lonely Knows Its Pain

"And can it be that in a world so full and busy, the loss of one weak creature makes a void in any heart so wide and deep that nothing but the width and depth of eternity can fill it up!"[122]—Charles Dickens

HOW near me came the hand of Death,
    When at my side he struck my dear
And took away the precious breath
    Which quicken'd my beloved peer!
How helpless am I thereby made!
By day how grieved, by night how sad!
And now my life's delight is gone.
Alas! how am I left alone!—George Wither (1588–1667)

"She who is truly a widow, left all alone, has set her hope on God" (1 Timothy 5:5 ESV). No more difficult or lonely transition in life is there than that of a widow.

What is the widow's loneliness? "Loneliness is not solitude, nor is it being lonesome," says Adrian Rogers, "or being in isolation. It is insulation; it is feeling cut off, unnoticed, unloved, uncared for, unneeded and maybe even unnecessary."[123] It is an internal emotion of pain generated by the lack of intimate connection with others. "Most loneliness," says James Dobson, "results from insulation rather than isolation. In other words, we are lonely because we insulate ourselves, not because others isolate us."[124]

> Loneliness…it is insulation; it is feeling cut off, unnoticed, unloved, uncared for, unneeded and maybe even unnecessary.—Adrian Rogers

Despite the many friends that surround the widow, there is a loneliness that is inexplicable, unspeakable and unimaginable, unless you have experienced it. An amputation has happened. He that was an integral part of her life; he that shared her laughter, tears, failures and successes; he that was her protector, sustainer and guide; he, her lover and constant companion; he that was her dearest friend has been severed from her life and is sorely missed. And that emptiness is torturous and agonizing.

Little comfort is found in chat rooms, group therapy and crowds. The absence of him is not negated by the presence of others. No wonder she is lonely.

10 Causes for the Widow's Loneliness

Absence of her husband

Eroding and evaporating friendships

Absence of close/intimate relationships

Fewer and fewer social invitations

Fewer connections (phone, text, visits, cards)

Withdrawal from and avoidance of others

Distancing from God

Emptiness

Feeling of being unneeded and unnecessary

Depression

Hints in Battling Loneliness

Loneliness is not always abated by moving into the home of your son or daughter or to another locale. In fact, the move may generate "secondary grief" and intensify it.

Loneliness is not remedied through medications. It's not a disease but a state of mind, therefore a pill can't cure it. Drugs serve only to complicate loneliness.

It is not resolved by companionship. The more, the merrier is not always true. Just being with people doesn't eradicate it. A widow can have acute bouts with loneliness in crowds. Neither is a full social calendar a solution.

Alone! Alone! All, all alone!
   Alone on a wide, wide sea,
And never a saint took pity on
   My soul in agony.—Samuel Taylor Coleridge[125]

"God's preventative for loneliness," says Neil Anderson, "is intimacy—meaningful, open, sharing relationships with one another. In Christ we have the capacity for the fulfilling sense of belonging which comes from intimate fellowship with God and with other believers."[126]

With the making of close relationships, engagement in meaningful social outings, increased interaction with relatives and friends (don't underestimate the power and value of hearing a close friend's voice to thwart loneliness), volunteering, attendance at church, and greater intimacy with Christ, the empty void left by your husband's departure to Heaven, in time, will fill (never though completely), thwarting the pain of loneliness. (Upbeat, positive music can boost the mood, lessening the impact and pain of loneliness temporarily.[127]) That which begins in a dark, lonely, broken place ends in light and delight for the Christian.

Ray Steadman states that much loneliness, weakness and emptiness is a result of isolation from the needs of others. He says that when we care for others without thought to our own needs and hurts, even those who have no claim upon us, we discover that there is "an accompanying wonderful sense of reassurance and an awakening of the spirit of joy in *our* own hearts."[128]

It was said to a widow of seventy-six years of age who was alone, poor and ill that her nights must be extremely long, always being alone. "If I were alone," she replied, "I should have been dead long ago, but I have a Friend who never leaves me day nor night; I commune always with Him, and His Word comforts me."[129]

That's the cure for loneliness. "Snuggle in God's arms when you are hurting, when you feel lonely, left out," says Kay Arthur. "Let Him cradle you, comfort you, reassure you of His all-sufficient power and love."[130]

Jesus, Lover of my soul,
Let me to thy bosom fly....
Other refuge have I none;
Hangs my helpless soul on Thee.—Charles Wesley (1740)

Billy Graham said, "God loves you, and even in the midst of your grief and loneliness, God wants to fill the empty places in your heart."[131]

16 From Widows to Widows

"Grief is like having broken ribs. On the outside you look fine, but with every breath, it hurts."—Unknown

Widowhood is a new road to travel, full of tumbles and falls, starts and restarts, dangers and detours. It's a road that will take time to navigate successfully. Good news! Help awaits (invaluable tips for coping with grief and continuing life) in widows that have walked the winding and treacherous path of grief before you. "While it is wise," says Rick Warren, "to learn from experience, it is wiser to learn from the experiences of others."[132]

Joyce Rogers

Joyce Rogers lost her husband, Adrian, of 54 years. In *Grace for the Widow,* she writes with regard to his death: "I have been on this journey so I can assure you that the 'fog' will lift. The piercing ache in your heart and the flood of tears will diminish. Jesus is the healer of broken hearts. He is mending my heart as I depend upon Him. If you hand your broken heart over to Jesus, He will heal yours also. I'm learning to take the journey one step at a time, leaning hard on Jesus. I'm learning to let Him fight my battles for me. Yes, the 'fog' will lift as it has for me. But life isn't easy. It will always be lived depending upon my Guide, the Lord Jesus Christ. I commend Him to you. If you hold on to His hand, He will lead you through the 'fog.'"[133]

"[And until] the fog lifts, don't try to think about what your future holds. Get out of bed, take a bath, get dressed, spend time alone with God, eat breakfast, clean up the house, walk the dog, pay the bills that are due—just do the next thing. Of course, pray all through the day."[134]

Elisabeth Elliot

Elisabeth and Jim had been married only twenty-seven months when he was killed by the Auca Indians. Jim was one of five missionaries killed while participating in Operation Auca, an attempt to evangelize the Huaorani people of Ecuador.

Elizabeth Elliot said, "We had been married twenty-seven months after waiting five and a half years. Five days later I knew that Jim was dead, and God's presence with me was not Jim's presence. That was a terrible fact. God's presence did not change the terrible fact that I was a widow. I expected to be a widow until I died because I thought it was a miracle I got married the first time. God's presence did not change the fact of my widowhood. Jim's absence thrust me, forced me, hurried me to God—my hope and my only refuge. And I learned in that experience who God is—who He is in a way that I could never have known otherwise."[135]

Elisabeth, speaking of the loss of Jim, states how the Lord gave her hope, peace and strength from the Holy Scriptures,[136] especially Isaiah 43:2. It was the first verse that came to mind in hearing of Jim's death and the one that kept her on the mission field. "When you go through deep waters, I will be with you. When you go through rivers of difficulty, you will not drown. When you walk through the fire of oppression, you will not be burned up; the flames will not consume you" (Isaiah 43:2 NLT).

In knowing the everlasting arms of a loving God enveloped and sustained her, she was able to press forward despite the grief, loneliness and pain. Her counsel to widows: "Christ is sufficient. We do not need support groups for each and every separate tribulation. The most widely divergent sorrows may all be taken to the foot of the same old rugged cross and find there cleansing, peace and joy."[137] Elliot said, "I've come to see that it's through the deepest suffering that God has taught me the deepest lesson...And out of the deepest waters and the hottest fires have come the deepest things that I know about God." [138]

Susannah Spurgeon

C. H. Spurgeon was the most famous minister in England. The Metropolitan Tabernacle, the church he pastored in London, was always full to capacity (6,000 seats) to hear him preach. He founded both an orphanage and pastor's college that are still in operation. Spurgeon is considered by most evangelicals as the "Prince of Preachers."

Charles and Susannah Spurgeon had been married thirty-six years when Charles died in 1892. Susannah's widowhood lasted nearly 12 years and was a singularly lonely one, despite the presence of her two sons and the many friends of her departed husband who sought to supply her needs. Grief did not keep her from the continuation of the work began when Charles was living (the Book Fund, the Pastors' Aid Fund, etc.). During this grief period Susannah wrote *C. H. Spurgeon's Autobiography, Compiled from his Diary, Letters and Records,* which took several years.

In the four volumes are chapters on the family life of Charles, written by her, where she cites the longing always to join him in Heaven. "Ah! my husband," she says in one passage, "the blessed earthly ties which we welcomed so rapturously are dissolved now, and death has hidden thee from my mortal eyes; but not even death can divide thee from me or sever the love which united our hearts so closely. I feel it living and growing still, and I believe it will find its full and spiritual development only when we shall meet in the Glory Land and worship together before the throne!" This was written in 1898. Compare the words with what she wrote in the Book Fund report (1891), and it is revealed that time and work had helped her develop a holy resignation in waiting for a longed-for reunion with Charles. "Oh! my husband, my husband," she wrote in the earlier year, "every moment of my now desolate life I wonder how I can live without thee! The heart that for so many years has been filled and satisfied with thy love must needs be very empty and stricken now that thou art gone!"[139]

> Oh! my husband, my husband, every moment of my now desolate life I wonder how I can live without thee! The heart that for so many years has been filled and satisfied with thy love must needs be very empty and stricken now that thou art gone!—Susannah Spurgeon

Susannah wrote, "For although God has seen fit to call my beloved up to higher service, He has left me the consolation of still loving him with all my heart and believing that our love shall be perfected when we meet in that blessed land where Love reigns supreme and eternal."[140]

Drawn from her experience, Susannah's counsel of comfort to widows is to live in expectation of a glorious reunion with their husbands (forever embrace that hope), articulate that anticipation, expressing heartfelt desires and longings about that reunion in a journal, and stay busy doing the Lord's work (through Susannah, Charles' ministry continued) until that reunion.

17   Things Widows Should Know

"You may never know that JESUS is all you need, until JESUS is all you have."[141]—Corrie ten Boom

25 Helpful Suggestions from Widows

Form a checklist of things to be done—a now list, a soon list and a later list

Get your house in order (budget, payment of bills, and investments)

Reach out to a trusted adviser for help with financial planning (removes the stress)

Don't bottle in the sorrow and pain; find a confidante that you can unload it on

The visits, calls and cards will dry up when it is perceived you are "over the grief" (Don't interpret that as unconcern or lack of caring)

Delay major decisions until the brain fog dissipates

It's okay to let people know when you need "private" time

The emptiness and pain caused by grief will soften over time

Build a circle of support (financial adviser, attorney, insurance agent, handyman, and auto mechanic)

The first two years will be the most difficult, with the second seeming to be without end

Open your mail, sorting it into urgent and nonurgent stacks

Have a family member or friend record a message on your husband's cell phone regarding his death, or simply turn it off

The loss of your husband means learning to live life differently, single

Don't expect anyone to understand what you are experiencing; they won't, because they can't

Give yourself grace to stumble or crumble

Connect with other widows who identify with your grief

Talk about your husband and speak of the memories as often as you want

There's no one right way to be a widow

Communicate what is needed specifically; the major need may not be a meal but taking Johnny to soccer practice on Tuesdays or having your car taken to a mechanic for repair

Say no to whatever is offered that you don't need (advice, invitation, etc.)

Refuse friend requests on Facebook from strangers

Stop caring about what others think about the decisions you make

Journal your husband's last words, wishes and the dreams he had for you

Safeguard your privacy

Don't forgo sifting through your husband's clothing and possessions; it's a wrenching but therapeutic part of grieving

> I live to show His power, who once did bring my joys to weep, and now my griefs to sing.—George Herbert

25 Helpful Suggestions from Others

Don't forget to promptly cancel unwanted auto-renewals (subscriptions, organizational dues), medical policies and the auto insurance coverage of your husband to save money

Maintain the joint checking account for at least one year to give time for refunds to be credited and checks and debits to post

To navigate the legal hoops of probate (probate is a court process that validates a will and makes sure its terms are followed), seek the help of an attorney who can relieve you of the stress and streamline it as smoothly and quickly as possible

Prior to securing the help of professionals, such as a financial advisor, tax consultant or attorney, vet them thoroughly

Formulate a new household budget based upon assets and income

Assign beneficiaries to your retirement accounts and life insurance policy

Order extra copies of the death certificate to close out accounts in which your husband was the sole subscriber

Regarding the emptying of closets and drawers, grief experts universally recommend not disposing of the clothing of your husband for several months, as it plays a role in the grieving process.[142]

Watch out for scammers and unscrupulous salespeople who prey on widows

Keep money matters private (reveal inheritance and estate assets only to the most trusted, and then only on a need-to-know basis)

Be prudent with regard to being a bank for someone else (family, friends, or in time a significant other may seek to tap your assets via loans or gifts)

Don't be overwhelmed when your network of friendship wanes (It is said that widows lose 75 percent of their friendships after their husband's death)

The initial shock and disbelief of your husband's death may resurface (holiday, birthday, wedding anniversary)

Laugh a lot—Timothy Faulk, Certified Trauma Specialist, states, "Experiencing humor and laughter daily is effectual in boosting the widow's overall mood and ability to deal with grief; Proverbs tells us that laughter is medicine, and this important emotion plays an integral part in the healing process."[143]

Mourn without murmuring (Exodus 16:8: "The LORD heareth your murmurings which ye murmur against him:…your murmurings are not against us, but against the LORD")

Rest sufficiently, exercise routinely and eat healthily; a well-balanced diet aids in the reduction of stress and speeds up the healing process of grief.[144] Get adequate sleep and rest. Consumption of caffeine late in the day may impede sleep at night (it takes eight hours for caffeine to be depleted from the body). Do some form of exercise daily. Walking, running, leisurely bike ride, or a harder workout "can ease agitation, anger, and depression."[145]

"Let your journey be what it is"[146]

Encourage friends to speak your husband's name and share their favorite reminiscences of him in your presence (Relieves those who are hesitant to freely speak of him)

Be careful not to use spiritual disciplines (prayer, fasting, Bible reading, etc.) as a technique to try to get God to do what you want. "If I do A then God will do B."[147] Attempts to manipulate God end in disappointment. Use the disciplines as an opportunity to be consoled, comforted and strengthened by God, not to obligate Him.

When the blackest of the darkness passes and the brain fog dissipates, clarity of God's design for your future will begin to unfold

Resume the functions and responsibilities of life as soon as possible

Don't allow your adult children to dictate the rules governing your future

Guide your children through their grief while not postponing your own

"Find your place in the 'Community of Brokenness.' Loss is a universal experience—but it doesn't have to isolate us. Though we enter this darkness of loss alone, there we will find others with whom we can share life together."[148]

"Knowing the Lord and His comfort does not take away the ache; instead, it supports you in the middle of the ache. Until I get home to Heaven, there's going to be an ache that won't quit. The grieving process for me is not so much a matter of getting rid of the pain, but not being controlled by the pain."[149]—Larry Crabb, about the death of his brother

18 The Grief That Does Not Speak

"Well has it been said that there is no grief like the grief which does not speak."[150]—Henry Wadsworth Longfellow

Articulating grief is hard—hard to describe its maze of sorrow; hard with regard to its deep and painful wounds that stubbornly resist exposure; hard for fear of misunderstanding or rebuke. But in order to heal, it must be embraced.

William Shakespeare said in Macbeth, "Give the sorrow words; the grief that does not speak knits up the o'erwrought heart and bids it to break."[151] Ron Dunn said, "[It] is right and essential to express the pain of our souls. Sometimes the suffering can be endured only when the pain can be articulated."[152] Allow yourself to speak of the cause of your husband's death, memories of his life, and the emotional roller coaster upon which you ride. Press yourself to talk freely of the loneliness, hurt, anger, fear, questioning and uncertainty experienced. "Words that express your grief," John Woodhouse wrote, "will speak predominantly of the good that we have lost. That is why we are grieving. Such words are appropriate and should be understood for what they are, not criticized because they overlook weaknesses, flaws and failures. Putting our grief into words helps us understand our sadness by helping us see its cause—the good we have lost—and thank God for the goodness, because it was His gift to us."[153]

It will result in a happier and healthier you.

J. C. Macaulay says, "Never allow your sorrow to absorb you, but seek out another to console, and you will find consolation."[154] It's as John Holmes said, "There is no exercise better for the heart than reaching down and lifting people up."[155]

Reactions to Grief

Behavioral reactions. Eating/sleep abnormality. Isolation. Disinterest.

Cognitive reactions. Disbelief, confusion, preoccupation with the death. Lack focus. Brain fog. Suicidal thoughts. Decision difficulty.

Emotional reactions. Regrets. Guilt. Numbness. Loneliness. Anxiety. Denial. Despair. Fear. Feeling "out of control." Hopelessness.

Spiritual reactions. The "why" question. Possible anger toward God. Doubts. Or unwavering trust in God is exhibited.

---

19 The Power of a Hug

"A hug is always the right size."—Winnie the Pooh

Hugs take the place of a thousand words. Hugs are arms enveloped with love and concern. Hugs are healing medicine when delivered by caring people. "Every hug helps dilute the pain."[156] Hugs express emotions too deep to speak. Hugs say, "I'm here and I care." Hugs say, "I wish that I could bear your pain and relieve your sorrow." Hugs bridge two lives together. Hugs are huge bandages for hurts and wounds. Hugs transfer hope and strength. Hugs are grease to the wheels of a broken heart. Hugs are spoons, and shovels that take a bit of our pain away. Hugs are consolation blankets. Hugs transmit happiness and health. Hugs instill calm and courage. Hugs speak what words cannot.

A Pennsylvania State University study concluded that "huggers are happier."[157] Additional research linked hugging with a diminished rate of sickness, stress, despair and depression.[158] The Bible illustrates the healing medication of hugging. The prodigal, upon returning home, was embraced with a hug from his father (Luke 15:20). It pictured acceptance and forgiveness. Paul, when departing Miletus, was hugged by his converts and coworkers (Acts 20:37). It pictured appreciation and gratitude. Jonathan hugged David upon revealing King Saul's intention to kill him (1 Samuel 20:41). It pictured love, support and concern. With arms outstretched upon the Cross, Jesus gave a hug to the whole world (Luke 23:33–34). It pictured loving-kindness, mercy and compassion.

Hugs that are efficacious are birthed in the heart (not from manipulation).

Hugs that are efficacious infuse comfort, hope, calm, courage, acceptance, love and gratitude.

Hugs that are (most) efficacious last from five to ten seconds.[159] *"Extremely short hugs" should be avoided.*[160]

Hugs that are efficacious allow the recipient to terminate the hug.

Hugs that are efficacious are not only the physical kind but also those that are written (text, email, card) and verbal.

Hugs that are efficacious are repeated hugs.

In your grief and pain, don't be deprived of touch. It's therapeutic. Part of the reason God gave people arms was to hug grieving widows, like yourself, in His behalf to instill comfort, calm and peace. Let them do it and be helped by it.

20   Soak in the Promises

In your grief, find hope in the promises of Christ, who has overcome death and promises you an eternal reunion with the one you love."[161]—Chuck Swindoll

Find strength in the Lord. Muse about His promises to care for and comfort you, and soak them in. In doing so, you will find that what Charles Bridges said is true. "One word of God, sealed to the heart, infuses more sensible relief than ten thousand words of man."[162]

Psalm 9:9–10 (TLB): "All who are oppressed may come to him. He is a refuge for them in their times of trouble. All those who know your mercy, Lord, will count on you for help. For you have never yet forsaken those who trust in you."

Psalm 91:1–2: "He that dwelleth in the secret place of the most High shall abide under the shadow of the Almighty. I will say of the Lord, He is my refuge and my fortress: my God; in him will I trust."

Matthew 11:28 (NCV): "Come to me, all of you who are tired and have heavy loads, and I will give you rest."

Matthew 5:4: "Blessed are they that mourn [grief felt at the graveside]: for they shall be comforted."

1 Thessalonians 4:13–14 (NCV): "Brothers and sisters, we want you to know about those Christians who have died so you will not be sad, as others who have no hope. We believe that Jesus died and that he rose again. So, because of him, God will raise with Jesus those who have died."

John 14:1–3: "Let not your heart be troubled: ye believe in God, believe also in me. In my Father's house are many mansions: if it were not so, I would have told you. I go to prepare a place for you. And if I go and prepare a place for you, I will come again, and receive you unto myself; that where I am, there ye may be also."

Romans 8:28 (PHILLIPS): "Moreover we know that to those who love God, who are called according to his plan, everything that happens fits into a pattern for good."

1 Corinthians 1:3–4 (TLB): "What a wonderful God we have—he is the Father of our Lord Jesus Christ, the source of every mercy, and the one who so wonderfully comforts and strengthens us in our hardships and trials."

1 Thessalonians 4:17 (ERV): "After that we who are still alive at that time will be gathered up with those who have died. We will be taken up in the clouds and meet the Lord in the air. And we will be with the Lord [and them] forever."

Joshua 1:9: "Be strong and of a good courage; be not afraid, neither be thou dismayed: for the Lord thy God is with thee whithersoever thou goest."

Psalm 23 (GNT): "The Lord is my shepherd; I have everything I need. He lets me rest in fields of green grass and leads me to quiet pools of fresh water. He gives me new strength. He guides me in the right paths, as he has promised. Even if I go through the deepest darkness, I will not be afraid, LORD, for you are with me. Your shepherd's rod and staff protect me. You prepare a banquet for me, where all my enemies can see me, you welcome me as an honored guest and fill my cup to the brim. I know that your goodness and love will be with me all my life; and your house will be my home as long as I live."

See *Appendix Four* for additional promises of comfort.

21   Getting to the Other Side of Grief

"Grief never ends...but it changes. It's a passage, not a place to stay."—Author Unknown

You know you're getting better when...

1. You have been able to say a final goodbye to your husband, until Heaven reunites.

2. Stuff that you both did together is becoming more comfortable to do alone or with others.

3. The ritual to the cemetery or crying on the way to work has stopped or greatly lessened.

4. You are interacting socially more.

5. Insomnia is less frequent, and a regular sleep pattern is developing.

6. You don't feel guilty having fun and laughing.

7. It's easier to face grief triggers (birthdays, holidays, anniversaries, vacation sites, etc.).

8. A new "normal" (transition to a life apart from your husband) is gradually happening which includes a new routine or schedule.

9. Memories that were painful initially now are pleasant.

10. You find yourself involved in helping other widows deal with grief.

11. The ability to focus and concentrate on something other than your husband's death is achieved. The brain fog that accompanies widowhood begins to lift.

12. You can sit in the church where your husband's funeral was observed without excessive difficulty.

13. The stabbing pain of sorrow is becoming less frequent (although it never disappears).

14. Apathetic indifference to the issues of life is replaced with a vitality of interest in living life to the fullest.

15. You honestly realize that moving on with your life is not abandoning your husband.

16. The automatic and habitual impulses that have your husband as their object no longer trigger emotional distress (remind you of his absence) as often or intensely.

17. You no longer dread the "empty house" as much as you did.

18. You are able to visit places and do things that contain no memories of your husband without feeling guilty.

19. Feelings of regret over things that you would have done differently had you known then what you know now are easing.

20. The "what if" questions no longer keep you awake at night.

21. Grief is abating, and you are able to think about your husband more as a happy past memory than a present painful absence.[163] The pain is not gone; it's just not as acute.

The light of smiles shall fill again
    The lids that overflow with tears,
And weary hours of woe and pain
    Are promises of happier years.

There is a day of sunny rest
    For every dark and troubled night,
And grief may bide an evening guest,
    But joy shall come with early light.
—William Cullen Bryant (1794–1878)

Should grief not be "complete" as yet, that's okay. You're on its timetable, not your own. Regardless of what is still to be experienced, the day will arrive when healing (to the degree possible) will be known. Until then, be patient with your grief.

22   When You Need a Therapist

"Whereas most grief dissipates on its own without support groups or therapy, widows suffering from "complicated grief" will find Christian therapy by a licensed therapist advantageous and beneficial to their healing."[164]
—Dr. Timothy Faulk, Trauma Specialist

    Complicated or pathological grief is grief that is unbearably painful, protracted or tenaciously blocked.[165] It's grief that goes awry, keeping the widow trapped in her pain and sense of loss.

    Normal grief resembles complicated grief during its first few months. The difference is that when the normal grief symptoms begin to fade, those of complicated grief linger or worsen, preventing healing.[166]

Signs of complicated or pathological grief may include:[167]

Unabating intense pain and sorrow about your husband's death

Focusing primarily on his death (obsession)

Excessive avoidance of reminders of his death

Intense pining for him

Inability to accept his death

Bitterness and/or anger regarding his death

A feeling of meaninglessness without him

Inability to move on and enjoy life

Isolation from others

Wishing you had died along with him

Grief recovery stalling

Deep and relentless depression

Pessimistic outlook (all is gloom and doom)

Significant loss of interest in the affairs of life

Suicidal thoughts

Questioning of long-held religious beliefs

Inability to have closure

Choosing the Right Therapist

Consult a Christian minister or Focus on the Family (1-855-771-4357) for a reputable Christian grief therapist in your area.

23   Anna's Counsel to Widows

"Others are going to find healing in your wounds. Your greatest life messages and your most effective ministry will come out of your deepest hurts."[168]—Rick Warren

The most renowned widow in scripture is Anna. After only seven years of marriage, she became a widow and remained so for eighty-four years. From her lengthy experience in widowhood may be gleaned several lessons for coping successfully with the loss of one's husband (Luke 2:36–38).

Anna gave her single state to God completely and wholeheartedly. Herbert Lockyer says, "When…God withdrew from Anna the earthly love she rejoiced in, she did not bury her hope in a grave. In the place of what God took, He gave her more of Himself, and she became devoted to Him who had promised to be as a Husband to the widow and through her long widowhood was unwearyingly in devotion to Him."[169] To gain peace and hope, devote yourself to the Lord unreservedly and totally, as Anna did. Abide in Him "day and night" in sweet fellowship and communion. Trust Him to be as a husband, providing provision to sustain you. Cast all your care upon Him to bear, for "He careth for you." Like Anna, discover Christ to be that "friend that sticketh closer than a brother."

Anna remained faithful to the house of God. Anna's seat in the church was always occupied ("day and night"). She found tranquility and hope in the fellowship with the saints and faithful worship in the house of the Lord for eighty-four years. Like Anna, every widow will benefit from the ministry of the church in four primary ways. At church your heartache and sorrow will collide with God's loving response. At church God's people will encircle you with encouragement and hope. In David's dire distress,

The Widow's Comfort

Jonathan 'strengthened his grip on God' (1 Samuel 23:16). Onesiphorus "oft refreshed" (encouraged, uplifted) Paul (2 Timothy 1:16). In the church there are many like Jonathan and Onesiphorus to minister healing to your wounded heart. At church the Word of God will minister counsel, consolation and coping strength to you, and worshiping there will be the means of refreshment, solace and inspiration. Is it any wonder, in light of these benefits of the church, that Anna resided within its doors for eighty-four years and David exclaimed, "I was glad when they said unto me, let us go into the house of the LORD" (Psalm 122:1)?

Anna didn't bemoan her estate. She didn't pine her days away in sadness and despair. Rather, she chartered a new course for life that would reconstruct her world, providing purpose, fulfillment and happiness. With God's guidance, set a new course with new plans, dreams and aspirations. Push yourself to rebuild a relationship with the world.

Anna prayed continuously. Matthew Henry says Anna "was always in a praying frame, lived a life of prayer, gave herself to prayer, was frequent in ejaculations, large in solemn prayers."[170] Cry out to God for divine comfort and healing of grief. David said, "The LORD hears his people when they call to him for help. He rescues them from all their troubles. The LORD is close to the brokenhearted; he rescues those whose spirits are crushed" (Psalm 34:17–18 NLT).

Anna expected the coming of Christ. There is no medicine to cope with sorrow like that of the hope widows possess of Christ's return, when they will be reunited with their husband (1 Thessalonians 4:16–17).

Anna spoke of Jesus. Invest yourself in the lives of hurting widows by sharing your story of Christ's sufficiency to sustain in the hardest of trials. The Bible says that God comforts you so that you may comfort others in distress and sorrow (2 Corinthians 1:3–4). Use your pain for another's gain. Billy Graham said, "Grief turns us inward, but compassion turns us outward, and that's what we need when grief threatens to crush us."[171]

Anna fed upon the Word of God. L. B. Cowper states, "God reserves His best medicine for our times of deepest despair."[172] Anna found the Holy Scriptures to be healing medicine to the crushed and wounded spirit, providing comfort, hope and coping strength. Psalm 107:20 says, "He sent his Word, and healed them, and delivered them from their destructions." Chuck Swindoll says, "In your grief, find hope in the promises of Christ, who has overcome death and promises you an eternal reunion with the one you love." See 2 Peter 1:4.

> In your grief, find hope in the promises of Christ, who has overcome death and promises you an eternal reunion with the one you love.
> —Chuck Swindoll

Responding to widowhood as Anna did enables you to gradually recover and be restored. Presently there is a hole in your heart that nothing of earth can heal or fill. Part of you will always be missing. But in time the fog will clear, the sun will penetrate the black clouds, coping will become more bearable, and the heart will learn how to beat again. Just ask Anna if that is not so.

24 Can Hardly Wait for Morning to Come

"No one has yet believed in God and the kingdom of God, no one has yet heard about the realm of the resurrected, and not been homesick from that hour, waiting and looking forward joyfully to being released from bodily existence."[173]
—Dietrich Bonhoeffer

> GOD knows how to make the night produce the morning.—A. C. Dixon

"Weeping may endure for a night, but joy cometh in the morning" (Psalm 30:5). In the morning the dirge of grief gives way to the joy of relief. A. C. Dixon states, "The night makes the morning. The morning comes and drives away the night, it is true, but GOD knows how to make the night produce the morning. Jesus said, 'Your sorrow shall be turned into joy.' Your sorrow shall be transmuted into joy."[174] Dixon continues, "GOD knows how to make the morning out of the night. He can touch the black charcoal into diamonds. He knows how to speak, and the darkness becomes light. The very affliction that would drag you down lifts you up; the things that are weights become wings. That which, if you could, you would have prevented lifts you up to Heaven."[175]

W. A. Criswell, long-time pastor of First Baptist Church of Dallas, was seated next to a well-known Christian theologian on a flight to a speaking engagement. The theologian shared with Criswell how his son of four years had recently died of a terrible illness. The father told Criswell that, knowing his son was to die, he did the only thing that he could do. He sat with the boy in a death vigil. He shared with Criswell how the boy's vision began to fade in the middle of the day. The child looked up at him and softly said, "Daddy, it's getting dark, isn't it?"

The father replied, "Yes, Son, it is dark. It is very dark." (And for the father it was very dark.)

The son then said, "I guess it's time for me to get to sleep, isn't it?"

"Yes, Son, it's time for you to sleep," said the father. The theologian told Criswell that he helped arrange the boy's pillow and blankets just the way he liked them.

The boy rested his head on his hands, saying, "Good night, Daddy. I'll see you in the morning." With that the little boy closed his eyes and breathed his last.

At that point in the story the father stopped talking and gazed out of the window for some time. Finally, with voice cracking and tears pouring down his cheeks, he said to Criswell, "I can hardly wait for the morning to come!" The grief-stricken father said that, knowing the indescribable joy that awaited in seeing his son in Heaven.

Do I hear you say the same?

I will meet you; I will meet you
    Just inside the Eastern Gate over there.
I will meet you; I will meet you;
    I will meet you in the morning over there.
—Isaiah G. Martin (1905)

Albert Barnes says, "The morning will come—a morning without clouds, a morning when the sources of sorrow will disappear. This often occurs in the present life; it will always occur to the righteous in the life to come. The sorrows of this life are but for a moment, and they will be succeeded by the light and the joy of Heaven. Then, if not before, all the sorrows of the present life, however long they may appear to be, will seem to have been but for a moment; weeping, though it may have made life here but one unbroken night, will be followed by one eternal day without a sigh or a tear."[176] "I can hardly wait for the morning to come!"

> One sweet solemn thought
>   Comes to me o'er and o'er:
> I'm nearer home today
>   Than I've ever been before.—Phoebe Cary (1912)

25   It's a New Relationship in Heaven

"We shall not know less of each other in Heaven; we shall know more. We shall possess our individual names in Heaven. We shall be known as individuals. You will be you; I shall be I; we shall be we. Personality and individuality exist beyond the grave."[177]—W. A. Criswell

Will we still be united to our spouse in Heaven in a marital role? Will my husband wait for me, or will he find someone else in Heaven? Jesus teaches that in Heaven believers don't stay married to those whom they married on earth (Luke 20:27–38). But neither will they be married to another. Marriage in Heaven is superseded by something far better—union with Christ (Revelation 19:6–9). W. W. Wessel states, "Marriage will not exist as it does now, but all life will be like that of the angels. This evidently means that the basic characteristics of resurrection life will be service for and fellowship with God."[178]

It's the marriage relationship that ceases, not the memory of it. The relationship will change, not the companionship.

Jesus' words do not mean that you will fail to recognize, reunite with or love your spouse in Heaven. It's the marriage relationship that ceases, not the memory of it. The relationship will change, not the companionship. By divine design it will be superior to that of earth, though this is difficult for the human mind to comprehend. J. Vernon McGee writes, "This doesn't mean that a man and a woman who were together down here can't be together in Heaven. They [just] won't be together as man and wife...[or] establishing a home up there, nor are they raising children."[179] "As children of God," writes Herschel Hobbs, "we will have a relationship far richer and sweeter than any we knew on earth."[180]

26   Clothed in a New Body

"There is a resurrection after death. Let this never be forgotten. The life that we live here in the flesh is not all. The visible world around us is not the only world with which we have to do. All is not over when the last breath is drawn. Let us cling to it firmly and never let it go."[181]
—J. C. Ryle

"Our earthly bodies, the ones we have now that can die, must be transformed into heavenly bodies that cannot perish but will live forever" (1 Corinthians 15:53 TLB). Look upon death like you do a builder that demolishes an old, tottering house to replace it with a better one. He removes the roof, the doors and windows and then pulls it down. But first, he removes its occupant. And after his departure, the builder builds a new and more glorious home for him.[182]

The Bible calls our earthly body *our earthly house*. W. A. Criswell comments, "While I'm in this house [the flesh], I can't have my new house. God has to tear down this old house first before He can construct my new house, the one made without hands, eternal in the heavens (2 Corinthians 5:1)."[183] This is what your husband experienced. He exchanged a temporal house for an eternal house. Your husband's new house is not a nonmaterial body, but one like unto that of the resurrection body or "house" of Jesus Christ. In the resurrection body, Jesus walked, talked, ate and was recognized (John 21:1–14). It was "touchable," therefore "feelable" (John 20:27). Therefore, be assured that you will see and know your husband in Heaven.

Why death? Jon Courson remarks, "Our present bodies of flesh and blood cannot move into the Kingdom because they're not designed for Heaven. That is what death is all about. For the believer, death is simply a way of leaving our earthly tabernacles [old house] and moving into our new bodies [new house], exchanging our crusty brown bulbs for creations of beauty."[184]

Regarding the death of your husband, don't look at the old house torn down, but by faith, the new house, the superior house "not made with hands, eternal in the heavens" (2 Corinthians 5:1). A man noticed a house with a sign that read, "This House for Sale." "How is this? Is the former tenant dead?" the man asked.

"Oh, no, sir," said the caretaker; "he has removed to a larger house in a better situation." In like manner, as we look upon the clay tenement in which your husband has dwelt, we answer, "No, he is not dead, but only has moved into the superior and permanent house in 'the better country,' a house not built with hands, where eternal life is."[185]

What a change that happens on "Moving Day" from this life to the next—the house of corruption for that of incorruption, that of mortality for that of immortality, that of the earthly for that of the eternal (1 Corinthians 15:53–55)! "When our bodies are resurrected," saith Adrian Rogers, "we will receive a brand-new body; yet it will be the body that He has already given us....Our bodies will be individualized with uniqueness, and we will know one another in Heaven."[186] What a transformation! What an exultation! What a jubilation!

27   Where's Your Husband and What's He Doing?

"If we could see what it is that happens to our beloved one when he leaves us—we could not weep!"[187]—J. R. MillerHelen Keller said, "Death is no more than passing from one room into another."[188] Paul said, "We are confident, I say, and willing rather to be absent [away] from the body, and to be present [Home] with the Lord" (2 Corinthians 5:8).

Your husband is living in another room.

No, not cold beneath the grasses,
    Not close-walled within the tomb;
Rather, in our Father's mansion,
    Living, in another room.

Living, like the man who loves me,
    Like my child with cheeks abloom,
Out of sight, at desk or schoolbook,
    Busy, in another room.

Shall I doubt my Father's mercy?
    Shall I think of death as doom
Or the stepping o'er the threshold
    To a bigger, brighter room?

Shall I blame my Father's wisdom?
    Shall I sit enswathed in gloom,
When I know my loves are happy,
    Waiting in another room?—Robert Freeman

Your husband is praising and serving God

He is seeing God in all His glory and majesty and magnifying Him. C. H. Spurgeon writes, "Mark the subject of Job's devout anticipation: 'I shall see God.' He does not say, 'I shall see the saints'—though doubtless that will be untold felicity—but, 'I shall see God.' It is not 'I shall see the pearly gates; I shall behold the walls of jasper; I shall gaze upon the crowns of gold,' but 'I shall see God.' This is the sum and substance of Heaven; this is the joyful hope of all believers."[189]

We can only imagine the thrill and ecstasy that your husband is experiencing in the presence of the King as he engages in praise and worship "night and day."

Further, he's busy with the job that was divinely assigned, some aspect of ruling the Universe. He's enjoying socializing with family and friends. He's experiencing rest (peace) from earthly cares, labors, pain and illness. He's praying that your needs will be supplied and your heart comforted in his absence. See 1 Corinthians 2:9. And with joy he awaits your arrival.

28   Good-byes Are Not Forever

"God transforms our hopeless grief into hope-filled grief. How? By telling us that we will see our loved ones again."[190]—Max Lucado

Good-byes are not forever.
>Good-byes are not the end.
They simply mean I'll miss you,
>Until we meet again.—Unknown

The death of Martha, the wife of President Thomas Jefferson, in 1782 left him so grief-stricken that he remained in his bedroom for three weeks. As a widow, you certainly can identify with that depth of grief. Historians tell us that Jefferson never overcame that grief.[191] What sorrow of sorrows that was for him to bear all the rest of his days—unimaginable!

No medicine is so effective in coping with intense sorrow as that of the hope of future life beyond the grave—a hope that Jefferson did not possess. Paul said it well: "If in Christ we have hope in this life only, we are of all people most to be pitied" (1 Corinthians 15:19 ESV). Anne Graham Lotz says, "Biblical hope is absolute confidence in something you haven't seen or received yet, but you're absolutely confident that whatever God has said is going to come to pass."[192] Max Lucado writes, "If you'll celebrate a marriage anniversary alone this year, He [Christ] speaks to you….if your dreams were buried as they lowered the casket, God speaks to you. He speaks to all of us who have stood or will stand in the soft dirt near an open grave. God transforms our hopeless grief into hope-filled grief. How? By telling us that we will see our loved ones again."[193]

In hope (the believer's certainty), we look forward to future life with our Lord and King in Heaven. We look forward in hope to exchanging the garment of weeping for the garment of praise. We look forward in hope to dwelling in a domain where sorrow, sickness, suffering and death are unknowns. And, yes, we look forward in hope to reunion with our spouse. It was for this reason that Vance Havner said in the aftermath of his wife's death, "The hope of dying is the only thing that keeps me alive."[194] Of Christians, David Jeremiah says, "When we view today through the grid of eternity, the sting of grief is dulled by His power and love."[195]

Chuck Swindoll says, "We will be together with our loved ones forever. What a wonderful hope! Paul doesn't say, 'Don't grieve'; rather, he says, 'Don't grieve as those without hope.' Grieving is okay, but your grief doesn't have to lead to despair."[196]

> Death has but *momentarily* silenced the conversations and companionship between your husband and yourself.

"The tomb is not a blind alley. It is a thoroughfare. It closes on the twilight. It opens on dawn."[197] Let this stir up hope and expectancy and consolation. Death has but *momentarily* silenced the conversations and companionship between your husband and yourself. A time will come when both will resume.

With David, lean heavily into the promise of life beyond death, saying, "My flesh shall rest in *[this]* hope" (Acts 2:26) and be comforted. Without it you will go to the grave with endless grief for all eternity, like Jefferson. With it, a peace that exceeds all comprehension will envelope you.

29   Get Ready for the Reunion

"Since no man is excluded from calling upon God, the gate of salvation is open to all. There is nothing else to hinder us from entering but our own unbelief."[198]—John Calvin

The only thing necessary to obtain abundant and eternal life, reunion with your Christian husband, and an everlasting state free from sin, sickness and suffering is to "come" to Jesus. Just "come"—not to the church, not to a minister or priest, not even to a book like this one, but to Jesus Christ. There is no need to do anything else to find hope and help for your troubled heart but to "come unto me."

Thomas Brooks said, "'Come,' saith Christ, 'and I will give you rest. I will not *show* you rest, nor barely *tell* you of rest, but I will *give* you rest. I am faithfulness itself and cannot lie; I will give you rest. I that have the greatest power to give it, the greatest will to give it, the greatest right to give it—come, laden sinners, and I will give you rest.'"[199]

"Come unto me, all ye that labor and are heavy laden, and I will give you rest" (Matthew 11:28). The promise, although certain, calls for response by "coming." How might you come? Come with a heart that is repentant (godly sorrow) over sin in simple childlike trust, receiving Christ's gift of forgiveness and abundant and eternal life through prayer.

Act Now

Use your own words—or, if you prefer, the following prayer:

Lord Jesus, I acknowledge that You died upon the cross and were raised from the dead to make possible my forgiveness of sin and rightness with God. I do willingly and eagerly turn from my sin to live unto Your purpose, plan and good pleasure. Jesus, this moment I do come trusting You to fulfill Your promise not only to rescue me from the plight of my sin but that of the grief of my heart. Amen.

In the world you've failed to find
Aught of peace for troubled mind.
Come to Christ; on Him believe;
Peace and joy you shall receive.
Why not now? Why not now?
Why not come to Jesus now?
Why not now? Why not now?
Why not come to Jesus now?
Come to Christ; confession make.
Come to Christ, and pardon take.
Trust in Him from day to day;
He will keep you all the way.—D. W. Whittle (1891)

The sun will shine; the sun will shine;
    The sun will shine tomorrow.
The clouds can darken but awhile,
    The sun will shine tomorrow.—Mattie D. Britts (1900)

Appendix One

Plan Ahead

1) Assemble important documents and store them together in one place (medical and life insurance policies, birth certificate, checking/savings accounts, Last Will and Testament, personal loans to others, user name/passwords to Internet accounts, and funeral plans). Make the location easily accessable and known to a loved one.

2) Procure a legal Will and Testament (or update it).

3) Acquire a living will (a healthcare directive).

4) Obtain legal authorization (a durable power of attorney) for another to act in your behalf should the need arise (disability, incapacity or death). Specify the matters it authorizes, when it authorizes them, to whom it authorizes them and its duration.

"When it comes time to die, make sure that all you have to do is die."[200]—Jim Elliot

Appendix Two

15 *Don't*s in Ministering to Widows

Understanding what to say and not to say to a new widow is challenging and deserves careful thought and prayer if it is to be on target to her heart with comfort. "Death of a spouse" is the number one stressor. No other event has a more potentially negative effect to a widow.[201] Bear that in mind in the sharing of condolences. Here are 15 *don't*s in ministering to the widow gleaned and adapted from articles primarily by widows.

Don't say, "I know how you feel" (no consolation)

Don't compare her grief with that of another (comparing losses brings no relief to her distress)

Don't assume she needs "space" (she may prefer company over aloneness)

Don't dump your grief story on her (at least not at the first)

Don't avoid talking of her husband

Don't volunteer to do something and not do it (pick up Johnny from school, provide a meal, run an errand, etc.)

Don't say everything is going to be okay (it may, but it's not presently)

Don't say, "You'll feel better in time" (provides no relief in the present pain)

Don't say everything happens for a reason (though true, it imparts no comfort in the immediate aftermath of her husband's death)

Don't say all things work together for good (as a Christian, she knows that, but with her eyes swollen with tears, it just doesn't infuse solace, which she needs from you)

Don't feel compelled to pass judgement on her decision to date again (part of healing for *some* widows is a new significant other)

Don't be a griever backseat driver (let her grieve how, when and where she needs, as long as she needs)

Don't say, "It's time to get over your grief and move on" (in truth no one knows when that time is except the widow)

Don't say negative things about her husband (this should go without saying)

Don't give unsolicited advice

Appendix Three
10 Appropriate Things to Say to a Widow

"I'll be here for you."

"I'm sorry for your loss."

"I can't imagine what you're experiencing."

"I am planning to prepare dinner for you Wednesday, if that's okay."

"My thoughts, concern and prayers abide with you."

"He will be missed greatly by me and so many others."

"It must be unbearably hard for you without him. I know you miss him awfully."

"I don't know what to say but wanted you to know I'm so sorry."

"I remember when he…" (share a story about him)

"I'm available anytime you would like to talk. I'm a good listener."

Appendix Four
Resources for Widows by Frank Shivers

Grief Beyond Measure, but Not Beyond Grace

Caught Up to Heaven

The Treasure of Grace

When the Rain Comes

The Wounded Spirit

Aging Honorably and Happily

Appendix Five

Psalms for the Time of Grief

Psalm 116:3–8
God will dry the tears of sorrow and grant recovery

Psalm 6:6–9
God hears the prayer of the grief stricken

Psalm 4:7–8
God restores joy and peace in the heart

Psalm 25:16–17
God delivers from trouble and loneliness

Psalm 61:1–4
Vent grief unto the Lord

Psalm 42:5–11
In grief, hope is found in God

Psalm 126:1–4
Deliverance from the captivity of grief

Psalm 18:31–36
Strength to stand firm on the slippery path of grief

Psalm 71:20–23
God turns ashes of sorrow into beauty of splendor

Psalm 20:7
Trust God with the future

Psalm 40:1–4
Be patient in the pit of despair—rescue is coming

Psalm 23
Comfort and consolation in the valley of death

Psalm 56:8
Tears are a language God understands

Psalm 27:13–14
I had fainted, unless…

Psalm 84:1–4, 10
Strength to stand found in the house of God

Psalm 55:16–18
Deliverance comes through prayer

Psalm 46:1–3
God is our refuge and strength in the time of trouble

Psalm 119:76
The unfailing love of God is your ultimate comfort

Psalm 32:7–8
God is the believer's hiding place in the season of grief

Psalm 121:1–2
Help awaits from the Lord, the maker of Heaven and earth

Psalm 62:1–2
Solace and repose are found in the Lord

Psalm 3:5–6
How to get a good night's sleep

Psalm 27:1
Fear is thwarted by faith in the Lord

Psalm 17:15
Death opens the door to eternal bliss in Heaven

Psalm 16:7
Divine counsel in the "night seasons"

Psalm 49:15
O Grave, where is thy victory

Psalm 91:14–16
The seven "I Wills" of God

Psalm 68:5
God's cares for the widow

Psalm 119:49–56
The Scripture, source of comfort

Psalm 116:15
Precious is the death of the saints

Endnotes

[1] Needham, George C. *The Life and Labors of Charles H. Spurgeon.* (Boston: D. L. Guernsey, 1887), 7.

[2] Spurgeon, C. H. *The Treasury of David: Psalms 120–150* (Vol. 6). (London; Edinburgh; New York: Marshall Brothers, n.d.), 403.

[3] Henry, M. *Matthew Henry's Commentary on the Whole Bible: Complete and Unabridged in One Volume.* (Peabody: Hendrickson, 1994), 2356.

[4] Osterweis M., F. Solomon, M. Green, editors. "Bereavement: Reactions, Consequences, and Care." Institute of Medicine (U.S.) Committee for the Study of Health Consequences of the Stress of Bereavement. (Washington, D.C.: National Academies Press, 1984).

[5] Adams, Jay E. *Shepherding God's Flock: A Handbook on Pastoral Ministry, Counseling, and Leadership.* (Grand Rapids: Zondervan, 1975), 136.

[6] Sittser, Gerald. "A Grace Disguised." http://www.growthtrac.com/dealing-with-the-death-of-a-spouse/, accessed February 24, 2022.

[7] Henry, M. *Matthew Henry's Commentary on the Whole Bible: Complete and Unabridged in One Volume.* (Peabody: Hendrickson, 1994), 2411.

[8] MacArthur, J., Jr. (Ed.). *The MacArthur Study Bible* (electronic ed.). (Nashville, TN: Word Pub., 1997), 1868.

[9] McGee, J. V. Thru the Bible Commentary: The Epistles (1 and 2 Timothy/Titus/Philemon), (electronic ed., Vol. 50). (Nashville: Thomas Nelson, 1991), 70–71.

[10] Larson, K. *I & II Thessalonians, I & II Timothy, Titus, Philemon* (Vol. 9). (Nashville, TN: Broadman & Holman Publishers, 2000), 221–222.

[11] Henry, M. *Matthew Henry's Commentary on the Whole Bible: Complete and Unabridged in One Volume.* (Peabody: Hendrickson, 1994), 2356.

[12] MacArthur, John. "Caring for Widows: Widows in the Church, Part One." https://www.gty.org/library/study-guides/209/caring-for-widows, accessed January 6, 2022.

[13] Langham Partnership Daily Thought, "The Hope of Glory." 11 November 2020.

[14] Spurgeon, C. H. "Precious Deaths." A Sermon delivered Sunday morning, February 18, 1872, The Metropolitan Tabernacle, Newington.

Endnotes

[15] https://www.azquotes.com/author/13978-Charles_Spurgeon/tag/joy, accessed January 17, 2022.

[16] Lucado, Max. "Every Life Is Long Enough," November 6, 2017. https://maxlucado.com/listen/every-life-long-enough/, accessed November 7, 2021.

[17] https://www.christianquotes.info/quotes-by-topic/quotes-about-death/, accessed January 28, 2022.

[18] MacArthur, John. What Happens When a Christian Dies?, March 12, 2006. https://www.gty.org/library/sermons-library/90-311/what-happens-when-a-christian-dies, accessed January 28, 2022.

[19] https://www.christianquotes.info/quotes-by-topic/quotes-about-grief/, accessed January 7, 2022.

[20] MacArthur, John. "Dealing with Sorrow." April 5, 2004. http://www.gty.org/resources/daily-devotion/DN462/Dealing-with-Sorrow, accessed March 29, 2005.

[21] Exell, J. S. *The Biblical Illustrator: 2 Kings,* Vol. 2. (New York; Chicago; Toronto; London; Edinburgh: Fleming H. Revell Company), 57.

[22] Havner, Vance. *Though I Walk Through the Valley.*

[23] Henry, Jim. *A Minister's Treasure of Funeral and Memorial Messages*. (Nashville: Broadman and Holman, 2003), 16.

[24] https://www.buschcares.com/blog/10-sympathy-quotes-for-someone-whos-grieving, accessed January 8, 2022.

[25] Lewis, C. S. *C. S. Lewis on Grief,* 10.

[26] Kreal, Michael. *Endings: A Sociology of Death and Dying.* (New York, Oxford: Oxford University Press, 1989). Kreal paraphrases Brown, 1945; Rodabough, 1980. https://silo.pub/endings-a-sociology-of-death-and-dying.html, accessed January 19, 2022.

[27] Meyer, F. B. *Abraham, or the Obedience of Faith* (Book).

[28] https://www.azquotes.com/quote/702861, accessed January 12, 2022.

[29] Exell, J. S. *The Biblical Illustrator: Thessalonians* (Vol. 1). (New York; Chicago; Toronto; London; Edinburgh: Fleming H. Revell Company), 175.

[30] https://www.azquotes.com/quote/598866, accessed January 12, 2022.

[31] Maddrell, Avril. "Mapping Grief. A Conceptual Framework for Understanding the Spatial Dimensions of Bereavement, Mourning and Remembrance." *Social & Cultural Geography,* Volume 17, 2016—Issue 216, 166–188.

[32] Spurgeon, C. H. "No Tears in Heaven." August 6, 1865. http://www.biblebb.com, accessed April 1, 2013.

Endnotes

[33] Kübler-Ross, Elisabeth. The Five Stages of Grief. https://grief.com/the-five-stages-of-grief/, accessed January 8, 2022.

[34] https://www.buschcares.com/blog/10-sympathy-quotes-for-someone-whos-grieving, accessed January 8, 2022.

[35] "How Do I Survive Losing a Loved One?," June 15, 2009. https://www.insight.org/resources/article-library/individual/how-do-i-survive-losing-a-loved-one, accessed January 9, 2022.

[36] Spurgeon, C. H. "No Tears in Heaven." August 6, 1865. http://www.biblebb.com, accessed April 1, 2013.

[37] https://kwize.com/quote/12499

[38] https://www.azquotes.com/author/10540-Max_Muller, accessed January 8, 2022. (The citation certainly echoes Christian theology, whether Müller embraced such or not, and is therefore included.)

[39] Wolfelt, Alan D. "You Must Say Hello Before You Say Good-bye."

[40] Ibid.

[41] Ibid.

[42] https://www.scribd.com/book/163599385/Healing-After-Loss-Daily-Meditations-For-Working-Through-Grief, accessed January 8, 2022.

[43] https://eterneva.com/blog/grief-quotes/, accessed January 8, 2022.

[44] Expressing Grief, October 04, 2016. https://www.insight.org/resources/daily-devotional/individual/expressing-grief, accessed January 9, 2022.

[45] https://www.christianquotes.info/quotes-by-topic/quotes-about-comfort/, accessed January 8, 2022.

[46] McKissock, Mal and Dianne. *Coping with Grief* (4th Edition). (ABC Books, 2012), 28.

[47] Neimeyer, Prigerson, and Davies, 2002, 239.

[48] Unknown.

[49] Yancy, Phillip. "Where Is God When It Hurts." http://www.christianitytoday.com/ct/2007/june/14.55.html?start=4, accessed April 14, 2013.

[50] Graham, Billy. *Facing Death and Life*. (Waco, Texas: Word, 1987), 163.

[51] Packer, J. I. *A Grief Sanctified*. (Ann Harbor, Michigan: Servant Publications, 1997), 189–190.

[52] Exell, J. S. *The Biblical Illustrator: Matthew*. (Grand Rapids, MI: Baker Book House, 1952), 57.

[53] https://whatsyourgrief.com/64-quotes-about-grief/, accessed January 8, 2022.

[54] Kubler-Ross, Elisabeth and David Kessler, *On Grief and Grieving*.

Endnotes

[55] Williams, Litsa. Grief and The Fear of Letting Go. https://whatsyourgrief.com/grief-and-the-fear-of-letting-go/, accessed February 21, 2022.

[56] Ibid.

[57] Ibid.

[58] https://whatsyourgrief.com/64-quotes-about-grief/, accessed January 10, 2022.

[59] Sager, Jennine. "What Makes Us Feel Better When We've Lost Someone We Love?," https://www.headspace.com/articles/grief-mementos, accessed January 21, 2022.

[60] Ibid.

[61] Beecher, Henry Ward, cited in L. B. Cowman. *Streams in the Desert.* (Grand Rapids: Zondervan, 1997), May 31.

[62] https://bestquotes.name/pin/103523/, accessed February 18, 2022.

[63] https://quotessayings.net/topics/the-sufficiency-of-christ/, accessed January 7, 2022.

[64] Graham, Billy. "10 Quotes from Billy Graham on Grief," September 6, 2019. Blog from the Billy Graham Library.

[65] https://hopeispossible.wordpress.com/tag/anne-graham-lotz/, accessed February 28, 2022.

[66] Stott, John W. *The Letters of John (An Introduction and Commentary.* (Tyndale New Testament Commentaries, 1988), 150.

[67] Hunter, William (1811–1877). "The Great Physician Now Is Near" (hymn).

[68] Alexander, J. A. *The Psalms Translated and Explained.* (Edinburgh: Andrew Elliot; James Thin, 1864), 557.

[69] https://www.goodreads.com/quotes/368087-there-is-something-you-can-t-fix-can-t-heal-or-can-t, accessed July 17, 2020.

[70] https://anchor.tfionline.com/post/tranquil-heart/

[71] Maclaren, Alexander. *Expositions of Holy Scripture, Vol. 3, The Psalms, Isaiah 1–48.* (Grand Rapids: Eerdmans, 1959), part 2, 61.

[72] From a quote by Martin Luther King, Jr., https://whatsyourgrief.com/64-quotes-about-grief/, accessed January 8, 2022.

[73] Ortberg, John. *Soul Keeping.* (Grand Rapids: Zondervan, 2014), 182.

[74] https://www.goodreads.com/quotes/274933-tears-are-the-noble-language-of-eyes-and-when-true, accessed March 10, 2022.

[75] Dickens, Charles. *Great Expectations,* Chapter 19.

[76] Meyer, F. B. *Abraham, or the Obedience of Faith* (Book).

[77] https://www.bartleby.com/348/1332.html.

Endnotes

[78] Dickens, Charles. *Oliver Twist,* Chapter 37.
[79] Unknown.
[80] Swindoll, Charles. *Insight For Today.* "Tears," June 23, 2021.
[81] Spurgeon, C. H. *Morning and Evening,* August 23 (Morning).
[82] https://www.stresslesscountry.com/valentines-quotations/, accessed February 1, 2022.
[83] Hagman, G. "Mourning: A Review and Reconsideration." *The International Journal of Psycho-Analysis,* 76, (1995), 909–925.
[84] https://www.wow4u.com/happiness-photo/, accessed February 7, 2022.
[85] "The Healing Power of Remembrance," https://www.modernheirloombooks.com/new-blog/2017/5/4/the-healing-power-of-remembrance, accessed February 1, 2022.
[86] Ibid.
[87] Wiking, Meik. "The Art of Making Memories: How to Create and Remember Happy Moments," *(Penguin Life).*
[88] Wolfelt, Alan D. "The Six Needs of Mourning," https://www.centerforloss.com/grief/six-needs-mourning/, accessed February 2, 2022.
[89] https://www.stresslesscountry.com/valentines-quotations/, accessed February 1, 2022.
[90] Ibid.
[91] https://www.wow4u.com/page8.html, accessed February 1, 2022.
[92] https://www.stresslesscountry.com/valentines-quotations/, accessed February 1, 2022.
[93] https://parade.com/1089418/kimberlyzapata/grief-quotes/, accessed March 9, 2022.
[94] Tan, P. L. *Encyclopedia of 7700 Illustrations: Signs of the Times.* (Garland, TX: Bible Communications, Inc., 1996), 305.
[95] Robertson, Frederick W. *Sermons,* Fifth Series, "Tears of Jesus." (London: Kegan, Paul, Trench, Trubner and Company, 1900).
[96] Anonymous.
[97] Lewis, C. S. *Mere Christianity.*
[98] https://eterneva.com/blog/grief-quotes/, accessed January 8, 2022.
[99] https://www.motivationalwellbeing.com/55-meaningful-quotes-about-helping-others.html, accessed January 3, 2022.
[100] Stevenson, R. L. *Treasure Island.*
[101] Wolfelt, Alan D. "You Must Say Hello Before You Say Good-bye."
[102] June 26, 2011. http://cslewiswisdom.blogspot.com/2011/06/relying-on-god-has-to-begin-all-over.html, accessed January 4, 2022.

[103] Graham, B. *The Heaven Answer Book.* (Nashville: Thomas Nelson, 2012).
[104] https://www.brainyquote.com/topics/tears-quotes, accessed February 14, 2022.
[105] https://parade.com/1089418/kimberlyzapata/grief-quotes/, accessed March 9, 2022.
[106] https://quotefancy.com/quote/1422486/Robert-Southey-The-grave-is-but-the-threshold-of-eternity-What-a-world-were-this-how, accessed March 16, 2022.
[107] https://gracequotes.org/quote/we-see-his-smile-of-love-even-when-others-see-nothing-but-the-black-hand-of-death-smiting-our-best-beloved/, accessed February 28, 2022.
[108] Parkes, Colin M. *Bereavement: Studies of Grief in Adult Life.* (London & New York: Rutledge Taylor & Francis Group, 2010), 6.
[109] Lutzer, Erwin. "One Minute After You Die," *Moody,* 1997, 59.
[110] https://parade.com/1089418/kimberlyzapata/grief-quotes/, accessed March 9, 2022.
[111] Howard, Henry. *The Shepherd Psalm.* (London: Hazell, Watson & Viney, 1909), 96.
[112] Lewis, C. S. *A Grief Observed.* (New York: HarperOne, 2001), Foreword.
[113] Graham, Billy. "God Always Helps Overcome Sorrow." *The Palm Beach Post,* May 2, 1967.
[114] https://parade.com/1089418/kimberlyzapata/grief-quotes/, accessed March 9, 2022.
[115] "How Do I Survive Losing a Loved One?," June 15, 2009. https://insight.org/resources/article-library/individual/how-do-i-survive-losing-a-loved-one, accessed January 9, 2022.
[116] https://www.encyclopedia.com/social-sciences/encyclopedias-almanacs-transcripts-and-maps/grief-counseling-and-therapy, January 9, 2022.
[117] "Hope Beyond the Hurt," June 15, 2009. https://insight.org/resources/article-library/individual/hope-beyond-the-hurt, accessed January 9, 2022.
[118] Eastman, Christie. "Twelve Myths About Grief." https://cabellhuntington.org/services/counseling-services/twelve-myths-about-grief/, accessed January 16, 2022.
[119] Graham, Billy. *The Journey.* (Nashville: W Publishing Group, 2006), 223.
[120] Lewis, C. S. *A Grief Observed.*

Endnotes

[121] "Common Grief Reactions." Hospice Red River Valley. https://www.hrrv.org/grief-support/common-grief-reactions/, accessed February 15, 2022.

[122] https://www.azquotes.com/quote/546337, January 27, 2022.

[123] Adrian Rogers. Dealing with Loneliness, https://www.lwf.org/sermons/audio/dealing-with-loneliness-1151, accessed January 27, 2022.

[124] https://www.goodreads.com/quotes/tag/isolate, January 27, 2022.

[125] https://www.bartleby.com/101/549.html, accessed January 27, 2022.

[126] https://www.sermonindex.net/modules/articles/index.php?view=article&aid=30585, accessed January 27, 2022.

[127] Raypole, Crystal. "12 Things to Do When You Feel Lonely," April 13, 2021. https://www.healthline.com/health/mental-health/how-to-not-feel-lonely, accessed January 27, 2022.

[128] Steadman, Ray. "The Christian's Tranquilizer" (sermon). https://www.raystedman.org/new-testament/1-john/the-christians-tranquilizer, accessed January 10, 2022.

[129] Exell, J. S. *The Biblical Illustrator: First Timothy*. (New York; Chicago; Toronto; London; Edinburgh: Fleming H. Revell Company), 236.

[130] https://www.christianquotes.info/quotes-by-topic/quotes-about-comfort/, accessed January 8, 2022.

[131] Graham, Billy. "10 Quotes from Billy Graham on Grief," September 6, 2019. Blog from the Billy Graham Library.

[132] https://www.azquotes.com/quote/459014, accessed January 31 2022.

[133] Rogers, Joyce. *Grace for the Widow*. (Nashville: B&H Publishing, 2009), Prologue.

[134] Ibid, 2.

[135] Elliot, Elizabeth. "Suffering Is Not for Nothing" (a message), *Revive Our Hearts Radio,* March 22, 2013.

[136] Gren, Lars. "Ramblings from the Cove," August, 2011. http://www.elisabethelliot.org/ramble/ramblings083111.html, accessed January 11, 2017.

[137] Elliot, Elisabeth. *The Strange Ashes*. (Grand Rapids, Michigan: Revell, 2004), 151.

[138] Elliot, Elisabeth. *Suffering Is Never for Nothing*. (Nashville: Broadman and Holman, 2019).

[139] Adapted from Charles Ray, *A Biography of Susannah Spurgeon,* 1905.

Endnotes

[140] *The Love of Charles and Susannah Spurgeon.* https://www.christianity.com/church/church-history/timeline/2001-now/the-love-of-charles-and-susannah-spurgeon-11633045.html, accessed January 7, 2022.

[141] https://www.goodreads.com/quotes/374714-you-may-never-know-that-jesus-is-all-you-need, accessed January 12, 2022.

[142] Nappi, Rebecca. "Late Spouse's Clothing Plays Key Part in Grieving Process." *The Spokesman-Review,* April 3, 2012.

[143] Personal Correspondence, January 18, 2022.

[144] "A Guide to Getting through Grief," March 13, 2012. Excerpted from the December 2011 issue of the *Harvard Mental Health Letter,* https://www.health.harvard.edu/blog_extra/a-guide-to-getting-through-grief, accessed January 17, 2022.

[145] Ibid.

[146] Wolfelt, Alan D. *Healing a Spouse's Grieving Heart: 100 Practical Ideas After Your Husband or Wife Dies.* (Fort Collins, Colorado: Companion, 2003), Chapter 3.

[147] Crabb, Larry. "Grief—The Difference Between Lamenting and Grumbling." *GriefShare.* https://www.youtube.com/watch?v=ejs4u9FQ0Pw, accessed April 21, 2022.

[148] Sittser, Gerald. http://www.growthtrac.com/dealing-with-the-death-of-a-spouse/, accessed February 24, 2022.

[149] Dunn, Bill and Kathy Leonard. From "Season of Grief, Journey of Faith," https://ritchilpgumpic.wordpress.com/2013/09/18/season-of-grief-journey-of-faith/, accessed February 28, 2022.

[150] https://parade.com/1089418/kimberlyzapata/grief-quotes/, accessed January 8, 2022.

[151] https://whatsyourgrief.com/64-quotes-about-grief/, accessed January 8, 2022.

[152] Dunn, Ronald. *When Heaven Is Silent, Trusting God When Life Hurts.* (Nashville: Thomas Nelson Publishers, 1994).

[153] *Moore Matters*, a publication of Moore College, (Newtown, NSW., Autumn 2011), 13.

[154] https://www.idlehearts.com/1870110/never-allow-your-own-sorrow-to-absorb-you-but-seek-out-another, accessed January 4, 2022.

[155] https://www.motivationalwellbeing.com/55-meaningful-quotes-about-helping-others.html, accessed January 3, 2022.

[156] Walton, Charlie. *When There Are No Words.* (Ventura, CA: Pathfinder Publishing, 1999), 50–51.

[157] Lucado, Max. "The Greatest Greeting in History," September 26, 2019. https://maxlucado.com/listen/the-greatest-greeting-in-history/, accessed January 16, 2022.

[158] "What Are the Benefits of Hugging?" https://www.healthline.com/health/hugging-benefits#How-many-hugs-do-we-need?, accessed January 16, 2022.

[159] According to researchers at Goldsmiths, University of London, longer hugs (5–10 seconds) were found to provide an immediate pleasure boost compared to shorter ones (lasting just one second). The influence of duration, arm crossing style, gender, and emotional closeness on hugging behavior, documentation stated in *Acta Psychologica,* Volume 221, November 2021, 103441.

[160] Ibid.

[161] "How Do I Survive Losing a Loved One?" Article Library, June 15, 2009. https://www.insight.org/resources/article-library/individual/how-do-i-survive-losing-a-loved-one, accessed February 15, 2022.

[162] Bridges, C. *Exposition of Psalm 119: As Illustrative of the Character and Exercises of Christian Experience,* Seventeenth Edition. (New York: Robert Carter & Brothers, 1861), 82.

[163] Understanding When Grief is Complete, https://www.mentalhelp.net/grief-and-bereavement/understanding-when-grief-is-complete accessed January 24, 2022.

[164] Personal Correspondence, January 18, 2022.

[165] "Mourning: New Studies Affirm Its Benefits." *The New York Times,* February 5, 1985, Section C, Page 1.

[166] "Complicated Grief." The Mayo Clinic Staff, Mayo Clinic. https://www.mayoclinic.org/diseases-conditions/complicated-grief/symptoms-causes/syc-20360374, accessed January 18, 2022.

[167] Ibid. (adapted).

[168] https://www.quotemaster.org/healing+others, accessed January 3, 2022.

[169] Lockyer, Herbert. *All the Women of the Bible.* (Grand Rapids: Zondervan, 1988). Chapter 2.

[170] Henry, M. *Matthew Henry's Commentary on the Whole Bible: Complete and Unabridged in One Volume*. (Peabody: Hendrickson, 1994), 1830.

[171] Graham, Billy. *The Journey.* (Nashville: Word Publishing Group, 2006), 223.

[172] Cowper, L. B. *Streams in the Desert,* 189.

Endnotes

[173] "Five Insights on Death and Dying from Dietrich Bonhoeffer," April 26, 2018. (Letters and Papers from Prison). https://www.hourofourdeath.org/five-insights-on-death-and-dying-from-dietrich-bonhoeffer/, accessed June 23, 2020.
[174] Dixon, A. C. *Through Night to Morning.* (Sermon No. 1), 1913.
[175] Ibid.
[176] Barnes, Albert. *Notes on the Bible.* (1834), Psalm 30:5.
[177] Ibid., 42.
[178] Wessel, W. W. *Mark.* In F. E. Gaebelein (Ed.), *The Expositor's Bible Commentary: Matthew, Mark, Luke* (Vol. 8). (Grand Rapids, MI: Zondervan Publishing House, 1984), 736.
[179] McGee, J. V. Thru the Bible Commentary: The Gospels (Mark), (electronic ed., Vol. 36). (Nashville: Thomas Nelson, 1991), 147.
[180] Hobbs, H. H. *My Favorite Illustrations.* (Nashville, TN: Broadman Press, 1990), 133.
[181] https://www.communicatejesus.com/post/40-quotes-life-changing-power-resurrection, accessed January 15, 2022.
[182] Adapted from W. A. Criswell.
[183] Criswell, W. A. "Grief at the Death of Family/Friends" (sermon), First Baptist Church, Dallas, Texas, January 12, 1958 a.m. https://wacriswell.com/sermons/1958/grief-at-the-death-of-family-friends/, accessed January 12, 2022.
[184] Courson, Jon. *Jon Courson's Application Commentary.* (Nashville: Thomas Nelson, 2003), 1090.
[185] Exell, J. S. *The Biblical Illustrator: Second Corinthians.* (New York; Chicago; Toronto; London; Edinburgh: Fleming H. Revell Company), 221.
[186] Rogers, Adrian. "The Resurrection Body" (Sermon # 2291). https://www.lwf.org/pdfs/2291-THE-RESURRECTION-BODY.pdf, accessed January 15, 2022.
[187] Miller, J. R. "The Beatitude of Sorrow," (1891). http://www.gracegems.org/Miller/beatitude_for_sorrow.htm, accessed March 28, 2013.
[188] https://www.thehealthy.com/mental-health/mourning-quotes/, accessed January 13, 2022.
[189] Spurgeon, C. H. *Morning and Evening,* January 10 (Morning).
[190] Lucado, Max. *Waiting for Christ's Return.* (Nashville: Word, 2000), Chapter 4.
[191] *Thomas Jefferson—A Film by Ken Burns* (DVD edition). The American Lives Film Project, Inc., 1996.

[192] Where Is Hope?, July 17. https://hopeispossible.wordpress.com/tag/anne-graham-lotz/, accessed February 28, 2022.

[193] Lucado, Max. *Waiting for Christ's Return.* (Nashville: Word, 2000), Chapter 4.

[194] https://www.christianquotes.info/quotes-by-topic/quotes-about-death/, accessed January 28, 2022.

[195] Jeremiah, David. "The Loss of a Loved One: Moving From Grief to Hope," https://www.davidjeremiah.org/heavenacademy/the-loss-of-a-loved-one?devdate=2020-07-17, accessed January 27, 2022.

[196] "How Do I Survive Losing a Loved One?," June 15, 2009. https://www.insight.org/resources/article-library/individual/how-do-i-survive-losing-a-loved-one, accessed January 9, 2022.

[197] Knight, Walter B. *Knights Illustrations for Today.* (Chicago: Moody Press, 1975), 93–94.

[198] https://www.christianquotes.info/top-quotes/20-awesome-quotes-salvation/, accessed January 10, 2022.

[199] Exell, J. S. *The Biblical Illustrator: Matthew.* (Grand Rapids, MI: Baker Book House), 224.

[200] Jim Elliot's Journal. https://quotefancy.com/quote/1175757/Jim-Elliot-When-it-comes-time-to-die-make-sure-that-all-you-have-to-do-is-die, accessed March 14, 2022.

[201] Help and encouragement for widows. By Staff Reports -May 7, 2021. https://www.dailyadvocate.com/2021/05/07/help-and-encouragement-for-widows/, accessed January 25, 2022.

www.ingramcontent.com/pod-product-compliance
Lightning Source LLC
Chambersburg PA
CBHW021018090426
42738CB00007B/822